The Soup Kit

Other books by Ginna Gordon:

The Lavandula Series
Based on the fictional journals of
Stefani Michel
  Book One: Looking for John Steinbeck
  Book Two: Deke Interrupted

The Honey Baby Darlin' Series
A serial memoir about cooking, love,
& the love of cooking
  Farm One: Bonnebrook
  Farm Two: The Gingerbread Farm

Sunny Mae & Bird in Alaska
  with illustrations by Dai Thomas

First You Grow the Pumpkin:
100 Cool Things to Make and Preserve

The Marriage Tip Book:
Advice from the Wise Ones of the 2nd Grade
with Nan Heflin

A Simple Celebration:
The Nutritional Program from
the Chopra Center for Well Being
as Ginna Bell Bragg, with David Simon, MD
Foreword by Deepak Chopra (pub. by Random House)

Visit www.luckyvalleypress.com

The Soup Kit

Ginna BB Gordon

Lucky Valley Press
Jacksonville, Oregon

Copyright © 2019 Ginna BB Gordon
All rights reserved

All photographs by the author

ISBN: 978-0-578-56623-8

Published by Lucky Valley Press
Jacksonville, Oregon

This book contains images and text protected under International and Federal Copyright Laws and Treaties. No part of this book may be reproduced or transmitted in any form or by any means whatsoever without express written permission from the author, except as permitted by law.

Book designed and produced
by Lucky Valley Press
www.luckyvalleypress.com

Printed on acid-free paper.

The Soup Kit
is dedicated to
Lee Gardner,
1952–2018,
whose friendship
was golden and whose
craftsmanship masterful

Contents

Dedication	v
Prologue	xi
Cooking Mentors	xiii
About Soup	xv
Cooking Basics	
Mise en Place	3
Equipment and Utensils	4
Knife Cuts	5
Mirepoix	7
Mother Sauces	8
The Spice Rack	
Borrowing from Other Cultures	12
American	13
French	15
East Indian	16
Mediterranean	18
Mexican	20
Chinese	23
Thai	24
Soup Basics	
Types of Soup	29
Flavor, Stocks and Broth	33
Thickening Agents	34
Protein & Vegetable Combo Chart	38
Basic Soup Kit & Plan	41

Chicken Stocks and Soups

First You Roast the Chicken	46
Clear Chicken Stock	49
Dark Chicken Stock	50
Other Uses for Chicken Stock	52
Soup of Consolation	54
Star Croutons	55
Chicken Noodle	56
Asparagus	58
Minestrone	61
Chicken Chowder	62
Thai Coconut	64
Avgolemono	66
Egg Drop	67
Hot & Sour	68
Wonton	70
Albondigas	71
Tortilla	72
Chicken Sausage Stew	73
Chicken Chili	74
Tom Kha Gai	76
Mulligatawny	77
Roasted Potato Leek	78

Seafood Stocks and Soups

Seafood Stock (Fumé)	82
Quick Fish Stock	84
Lobster Bisque	87
Cioppino	88
Bouillabaisse	90
Clam Chowder	92

Vegetable Stocks and Soups
- Clear Vegetable Stock — 96
- Dark Vegetable Stock — 97
- Black Bean — 98
- Heart Throb Café Bisque — 99
- Pumpkin Bisque — 100
- Butternut Squash — 103
- Beet & Watermelon Bisque — 105
- Chilled Cucumber — 106
- Creamy Wild Mushroom — 107
- Tomato Bisque — 108
- Broccoli Cheese — 109
- Gazpacho — 110
- Spinach Bisque — 113
- Miso Breakfast — 114
- Carrot Ginger Bisque — 115
- Acorn Squash Bisque — 116

Beef and Bacon Stocks and Soups
- Beef Stock — 120
- Dark Beef Stock — 121
- Texas Chili Con Carne — 122
- French Onion — 124
- White Bean with Bacon — 126
- Chickpea Stew — 128
- Potato with Chicken & Bacon — 129

Soup in a Jar
- Layered Patchwork Mix — 132
- Rice & Lentils Mix — 133
- Garden Vegetable Mix — 134
- Chicken Noodle Mix — 135
- Bean Mix — 136

Things to go with Soup

Legendary Cream Scones	140
Flatbread Crackers	141
Sourdough Crackers	142
Oatmeal Bread	143
French Bread	145
Dumplings	147
Warm Wild Rice Salad	148
Banana Bread	150
Compound Butters	152

Fruit Soups

Cherry	156
Fruit	159

Mother Sauces and Emulsions

Espagnole (Brown)	162
Béchamel (White)	163
Velouté (White with Cream)	164
Tomato	165
Basic Mayonnaise	168
Hollandaise	169

Misc

Tomatillo Sauce	172
Enchilada Sauce	173
"Curry" Sauce	174
Red Lentil Dahl	177

Afterword & Acknowledgements   178

About Ginna   180

Measurements and Conversions   182

On the following page: Tomato Soup

Prologue

"Eat what you want, just cook it yourself." Michael Pollan

Virginia's cooking, immortalized in *Bonnebrook*, the first book in my *Honey Baby Darlin'* cooking memoir series, was my bedrock of kitchen consciousness. From the get-go, my little three year old self was enthralled by the world of the kitchen. At Virginia's feet, on my grandfather's farm, I sat on a stool at the kitchen counter, doodling paper doll clothes, while my mother roasted chickens and made stock. She put my index finger on a mound of rising dough and said, "Poke it. Feel the spring? It's ready." She taught me how to rustle up dinner for a cast of tens; how to make jam and pickles and cured lemons.

On the farm, a big pot of something-or-other on the back burner added aromas to the kitchen. Today, I maintain those aromas: burbling stock, a ripe sourdough starter, a crock of pickles in brine are the natural incense of my kitchen. No week seems complete without a roasted chicken for dinner, turned to bone broth, soup, curry and salad.

Soup comes naturally to me: with an ancient fingerprinted recipe or a "Kitchen Sink Soup" made from this and that from the veggie drawer in the fridge. In summer, soup preparations are made for the freezer or cupboard, like frozen tomatoes and oven dried tomatoes and tomato sauce.

In fall, I long for soup, in winter we live on soup. I feel rich when the freezer is layered with bags of blanched vegetables, waiting to *be* soup. I feel authentic and healthy and righteous with containers of chicken and veggie stock in the freezer. Not to mention lucky.

But not everyone, including some very good cooks in my tribe of friends, knows how to make soup. 'Cause, there's a knack. Well, not a knack, because anyone can do it if you follow the steps. But the steps are important: when to add the meat, the beans, the roux. You can't just throw it all in a pot, bring to a boil and call it soup. Ok, you can, but this is better.

Begin with Mise en Place: "everything in its place." It is culinarily empowering to have the ingredients laid out and measured before you begin, so timing can be smooth and frustration limited. Nesting glass bowls, measuring cups, a sanitized counter: these and more are elements of Mise en Place a home cook can use to make the cooking experience more pleasant and economical, especially in terms of time.

If you have a stocked pantry, the essential ingredients, and a sense of Mise en Place, you can make soup.

In *The Soup Kit*, the information is laid out like a map, so you can follow recipes or branch out and put together your own memorable concoctions. From the proper equipment and utensils to thickeners, herbs and spices to units of measurement, even a chart of good protein and vegetable taste combinations, everything is here to help you expand your soup repertoire.

"Don't let corporations cook for you." – Michael Pollan

Cooking Mentors

My training as a cook began with Virginia's Leather Binders, carefully tended kitchen journals covering ten years of mid-western farm life. Virginia was kindled to cook by the Korean War, when my father shipped out and Virginia, my brother Mark and I were snowbound in Bath, Ohio. Flossie & Bessie, who held culinary court in the farm kitchen until my mother's arrival from California, were gracious and open-hearted, white apron pockets filled with sugar cubes for Molly the pony and tiny wrapped mints for me.

My 1972 edition of Edward Espe Brown's *Tassajara Bread Book*, purchased during my first visit to the beloved Carmel Valley monastery/hot springs in that same year, is falling apart. On pages 19–40, the general directions for basic yeasted bread, where each fold and turn of bread dough is diagrammed and laid out like a puzzle to solve, there are signs of use: butter stains, molasses fingerprints, brown sugary grit. The copies of *The Joy of Cooking* by the Rombauer sisters and *Mastering the Art of French Cooking* by Julia Child, both given to me for my first wedding in 1965, have far outlasted the marriage. Hard to believe their bindings are still intact.

Other key books on my kitchen shelf are *The Encyclopedia of Sauces* by Moya Clarke, *Silver Palette* by Julee Rosso and Sheila Lukens and Rodale's *Stocking Up*, which my father presented to me in 1969 so I could save us all by growing food in hard times.

I include Martha Stewart's *Entertaining*, beloved not only for its Martha-esque creations, but for the very fact that Steven Seagal's Rottweiler puppy, Willie, chewed the spine to bits when I was Steven's personal chef. Steven offered to replace it, but I declined; it's such a great story to tell, forever.

As one can see by my many quotes, Michael Pollan is my current chef guru, whose research and knowledge about real food surpasses all.

But, still, the two most significant teachers of my adult cooking life are the late Dr. David Simon, who gave me the best understanding of Ayurveda, particularly as it is expressed in the preparation of food, and Chef Gordon Smith, who arrived like an angel to help me out in the Chopra Center kitchen and became a friend and mentor. Chef Gordon's book, *Save the Males*, gives the modern (non-chef) man a view of cooking beyond ribs on the barbie and makes the world safe for any untrained cook. Gordon taught me much about stocks and sauces and made the intense 24-7-365 nature of the Chopra Center kitchen a lot more fun.

Chefs Ginna (Bell Bragg) Gordon and Gordon Smith
in the Chopra Center for Well Being kitchen in La Jolla, CA, 1996

"Eat real food. Not too much. Mostly plants." Attributed to Michael Pollan

About Soup

SOUP, GLORIOUS SOUP

Soup's been on the menu since animal hides and baskets of bark were used for cooking, with hot rocks to boil water and cook acorns and plants. A cauldron on a tripod over an open fire was the original crock pot.

The first example of a soup bowl was discovered in Xianrendong Cave, Jiangxi Province, China, and is thought to date back to 20,000 BC. The conquering Roman Empire brought gazpacho to Spain while the Chinese were creating wontons to be dropped into chicken broth. The 14th century European style of high, stiff ruffs around the neck made sipping soup from a bowl problematic, so they popularized the soup spoon.

The word soup, from French *soupe* ("soup" or "broth") comes from the Latin *suppa* ("bread soaked in broth"), and the word "sop" is a piece of bread for soaking up soup or stew.

The word *restaurant* means "restoring." In 1765 a Frenchman by the name of Boulanger sold "bouillons restaurants" or "restoratifs"—protein-based consommés to "restore" a person's strength. Most historians consider this to be the first restaurant.

And just so you know, in 1897 the first canned condensed soup appeared on the market. The soup was doubled in volume by adding a can of water or milk, or it was used straight for gravies and sauces.

It was a sad day when Virginia's fabulous cooking became, pardon the pun, diluted by the arrival of canned cream of mushroom soup into the Bonnebrook kitchen. For a time, it became the base for everything, from casseroles to gravy. Her cooking lost layers of flavor. Just sayin'… the 1950s were a confused culinary time in America.

Stone Soup

Once upon a time, long long ago, great hardship and famine had come upon the land as a nasty war (well, all wars are nasty) dragged on and on and on. One day, two weary, hungry and bedraggled soldiers arrived in a village asking for a meal, but the suffering people hid what they had. They greeted the soldiers on the village green and wrung their hands and bewailed their fate and said how sorry they were but they must decline to contribute, as they were half-starved themselves.

"Then we will make Stone Soup," one of the soldiers said, and asked only for a big cauldron and water to fill it.

"How mysterious," thought the villagers.

The soldiers set the cauldron in the middle of the village green and underneath it built a big fire. Then the soldier who asked for the cauldron whipped out a small bag from his cape, removed three ordinary stones and dropped them into the water with a great sweep of his hand.

When a curious crowd gathered, one soldier said, "A good soup needs salt and pepper." Well, that was not so much to give up, so one of the villagers sent his daughter home to fetch salt and pepper and a pinch of rosemary from the sidewalk bush.

Then the other soldier said to himself, rather loudly, "Oh, I do love Stone Soup, but Stone Soup with carrots... that's hard to beat." Another villager, overhearing this, sent his son home for a carrot from the cellar – it was just a carrot, after all. The boy returned with not only a carrot, but a big fat turnip.

"Magnificent, thank you!" exclaimed the soldier. "You know, I once was lucky enough to have Stone Soup with salt beef! Ah, that soup was fit for a king!" The village butcher waddled to his shop and scrounged around and found a little salt beef. And on it went, until soon there were onions, potatoes, barley, cabbage, and even some milk for the Stone Soup.

"A great soup would be good with a crust of bread and cider," a villager said, and went to his larder to find them. Now it became a feast, the villagers remembering this and that and the other thing to add to the pot and the soldiers sharing their beautiful Stone Soup with the villagers in return.

They all agreed they had never tasted anything so good, and they sang and danced and celebrated all night and all became fast friends.

The next morning the villagers thanked the soldiers for reminding them that, "Anything shared multiplies."

Ginna BB Gordon

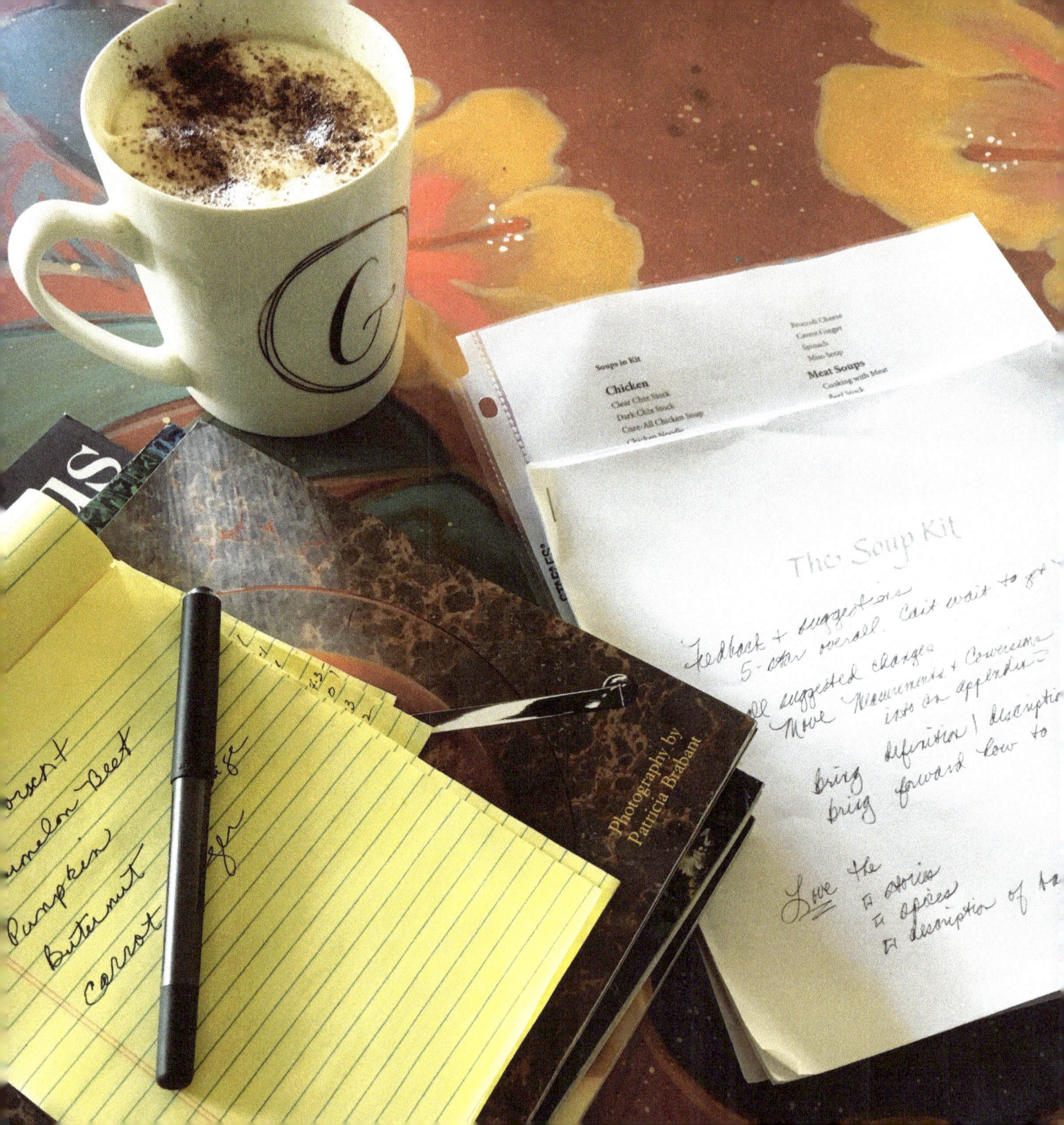

Cooking Basics

Mise en place pour la quiche, oui?

Mise en place

Professionals call it Mise en place; we call it making life easier.
— Glamour Magazine

Mise en place is the religion of all good line cooks.
— Anthony Bourdain

M*ise en place* (French pronunciation [mi zàn plas]) is a French culinary phrase which means "putting in place" or "everything in its place."

This refers to the set up required before cooking, used in professional kitchens to refer to organizing and arranging the ingredients a cook will need for the preparation of menu items. It's also a good practice in home kitchens.

The phrase is used as a noun (the setup of the ingredients), a verb (the process of preparing) and a state of mind, someone in the groove, well prepared and organized: onions or Mirepoix or other vegetable are cut, spices measured, broth portioned, pans and ladles laid out.

Mise en place includes sanitized counters, clean aprons and towels, clean sink and dish rack.

It also includes a clear unfettered mind. In my professional kitchens, we placed a covered shoe box with a little slot in the top outside the kitchen door, with this sign: "Leave issues here."

Equipment & Utensils

Knives
6 inch
8 inch
Chopper
Paring
Serrated
Sharpening steel

Pans
Stockpot
Crockpot
Frying pans
Sauce pans

Food Processor

Immersion Blender

Utensils and Tools
Nesting mixing bowls
Measuring cups & spoons
Wooden spoons
Ladles
Whisks
Spatulas
Tongs
Colander
Peeler
Sieve
Pastry scraper
Compost or Waste bowl
Timer
Pen
Felt marker for labeling
Painter's tape
Cutting boards
Sanitizer
Paper & kitchen towels

Knife Cuts

1. Julienne
The julienne is stick-shaped and thin rectangular cuts. Also known as matchstick cuts. Approx ⅟₁₆" x ⅟₁₆" x 2"

2. The Brunoise or Fine Dice
The Brunoise dice is the smallest uniform size for dicing. Bunch up your julienne cuts with your hand and cut the julienne into equally shaped dice. Approx ⅟₁₆" x ⅟₁₆" x ⅟₁₆"

3. Larger Brunoise
Approximately ⅛" x ⅛" x ⅛"

4. Batonnet
Start with squaring off the item, slicing it to the thickness desired and then going from there. The batonnet is used when serving a larger portion of an item, like a vegetable side. Approx ¼" x ¼" x 2"

5. Medium Dice
The medium dice is tiny cubes ¼" x ¼" x ¼".

6. Baton
A large stick-cut for crudites and presentation. It is the foundation for the more common Large Dice. ½" x ½" x 2½"

Ginna BB Gordon

7. Large Dice
The large dice is primarily used for stews, long-cooking dishes and Mirepoix in stocks. Approximately ½" x ½" x ¼"

8. Paysanne Cut
The paysanne is a slimmer, flat, square item, achieved by creating a stick-cut size and slicing thinly to produce a thin square. Approximately ½" x ½" x ⅛"

9. Chinese Diagonal Slice
Using a cleaver or a sharp, good quality knife, simply cut the vegetable on a sharp bias.

10. Chinese Roll-Cut
With a cleaver or a sharp, good quality knife, slice the vegetable diagonally, then roll it 90 degrees along the cutting surface, slice again, and repeat.

11. Chiffonade
The chiffonade is used when slicing very thin items like basil or leafy vegetables such as spinach. Stack the items you are looking to slice, then roll up the stack to producing a cigar-shaped roll. Slice the roll to produce a chiffonade.

Mirepoix

At four, I was busy making paper doll clothes and learning the art of a good soup stock.

"HoneyDarlin'," Flossie would say,
"Scrape these carrots – always have carrots, onions and cel'ry –
then add whatevah else you want."
~ from Bonnebrook

When I started rubbing white-jacketed elbows with professional chefs, I discovered that by instinct, Flossie was preparing a good *Mirepoix*, supposedly named after Charles Pierre Gaston François (C.P.G.F. to his friends) de Lévis, duke of Mirepoix, whose ancestors had been lords of Mirepoix in Languedoc since the eleventh century.

C.P.G.F. was himself an 18th-century Maréchal, or marshal, of France and an ambassador for the King of France, Louis XV. Lord Mirepoix's chef de cuisine (I wish I knew *his* name!) established those three sautéed vegetables as the basis for his culinary craft, and called it Mirepoix in honor of his not-so-illustrious patron.

As culinary legends go, this one disses the unfortunate Duke of Mirepoix as an apparently incompetent and mediocre guy… and who owed his great wealth to the deep… uhm… affection Louis XV felt toward the duke's wife. Alas, he really had but one other claim to fame: he gave his name to chopped vegetables.

Soffritto

A mixture of seasonings and finely chopped vegetables, such as onions, garlic, and celery, sautéed in olive oil and used as a base for many Italian dishes.

Umami

Savory taste term, coined by Kikunae Ikeda while studying dashi and MSG.

About Mother Sauces

A *Mother Sauce* is a basic concoction that can be easily varied. Initially perfected by the French, sauces are now universally categorized into five groups and referred to as the *Grand* or *Mother Sauces*. They are able to be prepared in large batches for use as a foundation for smaller versions that are then seasoned and flavored separately.

The Grand or Mother Sauces include:

Béchamel – a rich, creamy, smooth white sauce with a subtle onion flavor made by simmering an onion studded with whole cloves in milk and adding the infused milk (minus the onion) to a white roux.

Velouté – a rich, smooth, ivory colored sauce made by thickening chicken or fish stock with roux.

Espagnole – full-bodied sauce made with brown roux, puréed tomatoes and Mirepoix in a dark stock; used to make demi-glace.

Tomato – traditionally made by adding roux to tomatoes, veggies, and stock, today's tomato sauces are mostly thickened with a purée or reduction of the cooked ingredients.

Emulsions – Hollandaise, a smooth, buttery, pale yellow sauce made by whisking melted butter into a mixture of egg yolks, lemon juice or vinegar; Mayonnaise.

Recipes for the Mother Sauces begin on pages 162.

The Spice Rack

Borrowing from Other Cultures

Soup generally starts with a broth or stock infused with flavor with either vegetables or proteins or both (or stones!).

You can make a vegetable soup in any language and each culture makes that soup its own by adding the region's beloved herbs and spices.

Below is a good general herb and spice collection, and following that, some culinary favorites borrowed from other cultures. With these herbs and spices in mind, and *The Soup Kit*, the possibilities are endless.

WHAT'S ON THE SHELF

Herbs	Spices	
Basil	Chili Powder	Mustard, dried
Bay Leaf	Chinese Five Spice	Nutmeg
Chives	Cinnamon	Onion Flakes
Cilantro	Cloves	Paprika
Dill	Coriander	Pepper
Mint	Cumin	Sea Salt
Oregano	Curry, *see East Indian Spices*	Sugar
Rosemary	Crushed Red Pepper Flakes	
Sage	Ginger, fresh, crystalized & powdered	
Tarragon		
Thyme		

American Flavors

In *Eight Flavors*, culinary historian Sarah Lohman breaks down the history of American appetite into its component parts—starting with black pepper, and ending with Sriracha.

She leaves out coffee and chocolate because she says "they have been done to death," but the flavors she discovers as American come from everywhere else; a blend of Native American, English, French, Spanish. Of course! We are all immigrants.

Garlic

Curry powder
See Indian Spices, see page 16–17

MSG
Seriously. Monosodium Glutamate, discovered by Kikunae Ikeda, a University of Tokyo chemistry professor, while studying the intense flavors of dashi, a Japanese seaweed broth known for its intense flavor. He is given credit for the term Umami.

Black pepper
The number one selling spice in America.

Soy Sauce
Originally imported by the East India Company from Britain by way of China.

Chili Powder

Vanilla
The United States is the largest importer of vanilla in the world.

Sriracha

Due to the constant threat of bombing in South Vietnam during the Vitenam war, chili peppers were difficult to harvest and sell, so a family of chili farmers made a sauce which became an instant hit with the locals and the Americans used it to spice up army rations.

The above breakdown clearly shows the dependency of the USA on flavors from other cultures—nothing on the list of eight flavors originated in US or in its young culture. It also shows the average American's (that is, North American's, that is United States-ian's) reliance on packaged, processed and pre-made food.

In my world, the American cooks who inspire me, cook from scratch, relying as little as possible on processed foods. Borrowing from other cultures? Sure. But, rather than curry powder (see *Indian Flavors, page 16*), pop cumin seeds in ghee; instead of MSG, herb and spice combos emerge; rather than chili powder, use roast peppers and chop fresh tomatoes in season and make salsa.

My friend, Elsa, grew up in Mexico. She says she can taste the real or packaged flavors of her country in various situations: at a local Mexican restaurant, everthing tasted canned. She shook her head... "No." My Enchilada Sauce, however, caused her to utter the now much quoted line: "These flavors go all the way through."

I love that.

It's simple—roast the chicken, roast the peppers, make the stock, use fresh everything, You don't have to stay home all day every day to cook from scratch. It's not that hard. It takes a little devotion, self education and an attitude of self-care in the kitchen.

French Flavors

Fines Herbes:
These include tarragon, chives, chervil and parsley; fine referring to their delicate flavors, added at the end of cooking a dish, as opposed to *robust* French herbs (oregano, marjoram, rosemary and thyme) which are cooked within.

Persillade
A mixture of chopped parsley and garlic (and sometimes oil and vinegar), cooked or added raw at the end of cooking. This is a classic addition to roasted potatoes.

Herbes de Provence
A Provençal mixture of marjoram, rosemary, thyme, oregano, and lavender, for meat, fowl, fish, soups and stews.

Nutmeg
Adds nuttiness and fragrance to sauces, such as béchamel, and desserts, like pain d'épices.

Tarragon
A licorice-flavored herb used in cooking poultry and seafood, and to infuse vinegar and flavor mustard.

Saffron
"The most expensive spice in the world," used in Mediterranean seafood dishes, such as Bouillabaisse, of Southern France.

Bouquet Garni
Usually consisting of sage, parsley, thyme, bay leaf and peppercorns tied together with string or wrapped in a cheesecloth, the "garnished bouquet" is used to flavor soups and stocks.

East Indian Flavors

An Indian *savory* spice mix commonly known as *Curry Powder* is a British corruption of the Tamil or Sanskrit word for sauce, "kari." In other words, in India there is no such thing as curry powder.

The *sweet* spice is known as **Garam Masala** in northern India and **Bese Bel** in the south.

To make Indian spice mixes, the three most important ingredients are *coriander, cumin and mustard seeds*.

Buy spices whole when possible, because after grinding a spice it begins to lose its pungency and aroma.

To release the flavor, the whole spices need to be lightly dry-fried before crushing to a powder:

Place seeds in a small frying pan over a medium heat and stir until seeds begin to pop and give off their fragrant aroma.

Take off the heat and spread on a plate, as they will continue to cook in a hot frying pan and will easily burn.

Always dry fry coriander and cumin separately as cumin fries much quicker than coriander.

Mustard seeds will also go into your savory spice mix and are added during tempering: add spices to hot oil and cook until the mustard seeds pop, releasing their wonderful heat and flavor into the oil.

The Soup Kit

Savory "Curry Powder"

a traditional savory blend

1 tbsp whole coriander seeds

1 tbsp whole cumin seeds

1 tsp whole black peppercorns

1 tsp whole brown mustard seeds

1 tsp whole fenugreek seeds

3 hot dried red chilies, crumbled

½ tsp ground turmeric

Dry fry all the spices except the turmeric until fragrant, but don't let them brown as it will ruin the flavor. Add the turmeric and quickly stir. Cool on a plate. Then grind as finely as possible. Store in an airtight container.

Garam Masala Powder

an aromatic sweet blend

1 tbsp cardamom seeds

1 tsp whole cloves

1 tsp black peppercorns

1 stick of cinnamon

¼ tsp of nutmeg

a curl of mace

1 small dried chili

6 curry leaves

1 tbsp unsweetened coconut flakes

Dry-fry all the spices until fragrant, remove from heat and add coconut flakes. Grind as finely as possible. Store in an airtight container.

See page 174 for a Curry Sauce recipe.

Mediterranean Flavors

Allspice

Allspice takes its name from its aroma, which smells like a combination of spices, especially cinnamon, cloves, ginger and nutmeg. In much of the world, allspice is called pimento because the Spanish mistook the fruit for black pepper, which the Spanish called pimienta. See also *Mexican Flavors*.

Basil

Cardamom

Cilantro

Coriander

Cumin

Nutmeg

Oregano

Paprika

Parsley

Rosemary

Saffron

Sumac

Sumac powder has a very nice, fruity-tart flavor which is not quite as overpowering as lemon.

Thyme

Turmeric

Za'atar

Za'atar Spice is a blend of savory dried herbs like oregano, marjoram or thyme, and earthy spices like cumin and coriander, with sesame seeds, salt and the most important ingredient of all… sumac!

Mexican Flavors

Achiote
The orange-red seeds of the annatto tree, native to the tropical areas of the Americas, dried and ground to a powder or made into a paste. Its flavor is sweet and earthy, pairs well with citrus.

Allspice
The dried unripe fruit of the pimento dioica tree, native to Southern Mexico, the Caribbean, and Central America. It has the flavor of cinnamon, ginger, clove, and nutmeg combined.

Anise
The seed of a flowering plant native to the eastern Mediterranean region and Southeast Asia, something like licorice, fennel or tarragon. It pairs well with cinnamon and vanilla. In Mexico, it is used mainly in cakes, cookies and sweet breads and is one of the ingredients of molé.

Dried Chilies
To make savory dishes, use whole dried chilies. Chili powder is a quick substitute.

Cinnamon
The dried inner bark of several species of cinnamom trees.

Clove
The flower buds of an evergreen tree native to Indonesia, paired with cumin and cinnamon in savory dishes. Used in baked goods and to flavor molés.

Coriander
The whole dried seeds of the cilantro plant with a floral, citrusy, and sweet flavor, pairs well with cumin, thyme, and black pepper. Used to flavor chorizo and soups and stews.

Cumin
The seed of a flowering plant native to the East Mediterranean and South Asia with a strong earthy and bitter flavor, pairs well with coriander and dried chilies. Used in sauce and stews.

Epazoté
While technically an herb, epazoté in its dry form is used as a spice. Native to Mexico and Central and South America. It is pungent with notes of anise, oregano, citrus, and mint. Used in sauces.

Mexican Bay leaf
The dried leaves of an evergreen shrub native to Mexico; slightly floral, herbal, and a bit bitter, similar to oregano and marjoram. Used in soups, stews, broths, and rice.

Mexican Oregano
The flowering plant in the verbena family native to the Southern United States, Mexico, and Central America, a pungent flavor with hints of licorice and citrus. It pairs well with paprika, cumin, and chili peppers. In Mexican cuisine, used to flavor beans, soups, and stews.

Vanilla

The pod of a flowering vine in the orchid family native to Mexico and South America. Its flavor is sweet, yet smoky. It is often paired with cinnamon and clove. In Mexico, it is used extensively in desserts like flan, ice cream, cake, and to make hot chocolate. You can also find it in savory dishes, especially in the Veracruz region.

Legend has it that Totonac princess, Tzacopontziza, fell in love with prince Zkatan-Oxga, although she was destined to live a life consecrated to the goddess Tonacayohua. The punishment of seducing a princess promised to the goddess was death so off they escaped to the mountains, but were later found and killed by the high priests. A large bush grew where their blood was spilled, which later intertwined with a vine, which flowered into a beautiful orchid plant.

The Totonac believed the orchid and the shrub were the two lovers. The flowers became pods and released their aroma, which led to vanilla.

Chinese Flavors

Ginger

Garlic

Star Anise

Star anise is not the same thing as aniseed. It's the fruit of a small evergreen tree in Mongolia. The fruit is picked green and dried until it resembles a hard, nut-brown seed, with six to ten points on the star, each containing a single seed.

The pungent, licorice-like aroma makes star anise an integral ingredient in Chinese five spice, combined with fennel, cinnamon, Szechuan peppercorns and cloves. This spice is used to season everything from roast duck to spiced nuts.

Cloves

Chili

5-spice powder

A blend of cinnamon, cloves, fennel, star anise, and Szechwan peppercorns

Chinese Cinnamon

Scallions

Sesame Seeds

Black Pepper

Fennel Seeds

Thai Flavors

Basil

Cinnamon

Bird Chili
   The smallest of the chilies, and the hottest.

Chili
   Not as hot as the bird chili.

Citron
   A round dark green fruit. Sour orange juice and orange peel can be substituted.

Cloves
   The dried flower buds of an evergreen tree native to the Molucca Islands.

Cumin

Ginger

Garlic

Coconut

I'll stop here with spice combinations.

On the following page: <u>Soup of Consolation</u>

Soup Basics

Mushroom Bisque, Red Lentil Dahl, Chicken Pesto Noodle, White Bean with Bacon

Types of Soup

CLEAR SOUPS

Clear Soup is light or mild-flavored, including broths and bouillons from meats, poultry, game, fish or vegetables.

Broth

Like stocks, broths are prepared by simmering ingredients in a liquid over a long period of time. The differences between a broth and stock are: a broth uses meat (a finished broth can be served as is) and stocks are primarily bones and are bases for soups, sauces and flavoring.

Broth-Based Vegetable Soup

Broth-based vegetable soup, in which the vegetables and meats are cooked directly in the broth, adds flavor, body and texture to the finished product.

Consommés

A consommé is one of the more complicated types of soup to create. A consommé starts with a good stock, clarified by simmering gently with ingredients that attract the clouding particles. In order to make a proper consommé, you have to be able to produce a *raft*.

Among the flavoring ingredients used are Mirepoix, tomatoes and browned onion, egg whites and ground meat the same as the stock (Ground chicken for chicken stock, ground beef for beef stock, etc.). These ingredients are simmered with the stock and egg whites to form the *raft*.

Breaking this raft by boiling or poking will cause the entire process to fail. The idea is to be gentle so the particles picked up by the consommé raft aren't agitated back into the stock.

Stock has impurities within the broth, bits of meat or collagen normally no problem as stocks are there for flavor and those bits are full of flavor. Clarity is the desirable trait of any consommé.

The consommé is carefully strained through several layers of cheesecloth to remove any bits. It is completely degreased by cooling and refrigerating then removing the solidified fat.

THICK SOUPS

Thickening soup can be done by a roux *(see page 36)*, starch from potatoes or rice, a cream reduction, or by a mother sauce such as a velouté *(see page 164)*.

Using a roux creates a smooth, even texture as the roux is cooked along with the vegetables and then the stock is slowly added, whisking constantly to avoid lumps until all liquid has been used. As the soup warms, it will thicken.

Cream-based Soup Basics

Sweat Mirepoix with firm chopped vegetables of choice in butter or oil. Do not brown.

If using stock, sprinkle flour on vegetables and cook to a white roux stage *(see page 36)*, then add hot stock. Or add a velouté *(page 164)* and bring to a boil.

Simmer approximately 30 to 40 minutes to cook the roux and flavoring vegetables. Skim if needed. If including leafy greens, add them in the last 10 minutes.

Strain the soup into a clean pot and purée. Bring the soup back to a simmer.

Finish the soup with the hot cream or bechamel.

Puréed Soup Basics

Cook starchy vegetables or legumes (or both!) in a stock or broth and purée the ingredients. When puréeing add a portion of the liquid slowly to get the desired thickness.

Puréed soups generally do not use additional thickeners, like roux or whitewash (*see page 34*). The natural starches in the main ingredients give the thickening power.

Bisque Basics

In the old days, bisques were made from shellfish or game and thickened with cooked rice and pulverized shells or bones. Modern bisques use a combination of cream and purée, no pulverized shells, and simmering for long time periods. Roux is the preferred thickener, producing a smooth-textured soup.

The term bisque is often used to describe puréed vegetable soups (Butternut Squash, for example) enriched with cream and butter.

Chowders

The Breton phrase *faire chaudiere* means "to make a fish stew in a cauldron." Chowders are hearty soups with chunks of the main ingredients (usually diced potatoes) and garnishes. Most chowders are thickened with roux.

Render finely diced salt pork over medium heat.

Sweat Mirepoix in the rendered pork.

Add flour to make a roux.

Add the liquid.

Add the seasoning and flavoring ingredients according to their cooking times.

Simmer, skimming as needed.

Add milk or cream.

COLD SOUPS

Cold soups can be chilled versions of cream soups or as unique as a cold fruit soup.

Cooked Cold Soups

Vichyssoise, a popular cold soup, is cold potato-leek soup, puréed. If the soup is to be creamed, add the cream just before serving. This extends the soup's shelf life.

Cold soups should have a thinner consistency than hot soups, less thickener or more liquid. Serve cold soups as cold as possible.

Uncooked Cold Soups

In uncooked cold soups the puréed fruits or vegetables add thickness, body and flavor. Add cold stock or juice to adjust the soup's consistency. Cream, sour cream, crème fraîche or yogurt are added to enrich the soup.

Prepare small batches as close to serving time as possible, as enzymes and bacteria are not destroyed by cooking and uncooked soup spoils more quickly!

Flavor, Stocks, & Broths

Making stock at home is important for the gelatin content extracted from bones; most commercially available stocks lack the "jelly."

Traditional stocks are made with collagen rich bones like knuckles, necks and backs. When moisture and heat are applied, the collagen breaks down, creating the gelatin, or jelly.

Bones contain a lot of collagen but less flavor. For a truly flavorful stock, add meat.

You need an extremely flavorful stock when making consommé because the clarification process will extract both gelatin and flavor.

For a full flavored chicken consommé, you can make a "double stock:" cut up a whole chicken, bones and all, and make a white or roasted chicken stock. Strain the stock and make a new stock with another whole chicken, using the first stock instead of water.

Thickening Agents

Most thickening agent, except a Reduction, are some kind of starch which becomes gelatinous when cooked. Simple enough.

Liaison

A liaison is a mixture of egg yolks and cream to finish some of the classical French sauces. A liaison will slightly thicken a sauce, but its biggest contribution is a richness in flavor.

Pure egg yolks curdle around 140–150° F or 60–70° C. When egg yolks are mixed with cream, the curdling temperature raises to 180–185° F or 83° C.

A liaison thickening agent is more about the smoothness and richness and less about actual thickening. Add a little hot liquid to the egg mixture before adding to the soup. Ratio is generally 3 yolks to 7 fl. oz cream.

Arrowroot

Arrowroot is derived from several tropical plants and is similar to cornstarch in texture, appearance and thickening power and is used in the same way. Arrowroot produces a clearer finished product than cornstarch and and doesn't break down as quickly.

Beurre Manie

Beurre Manie is a combination of equal parts flour and softened butter kneaded together and formed into tiny balls to be dropped into sauces for flavor and thickening at the end of the cooking process. The butter adds shine and flavor as it melts. *See* Roux.

Whitewash

A whitewash is a mixture of flour and water. The mixed liquid is added to a soup or a sauce. Flour adds a bit of flavor and might separate from what it was thickening if cooked too long. A whitewash is best when you need to thicken a dish just before serving.

Cornstarch Slurry

Same as a whitewash, except uses cornstarch instead of flour. Cornstarch is mixed with water and added to the soup/sauce. The proper technique is to add a cold slurry to a hot liquid while stirring. It takes longer to gelatinize than flour.

Reduction

Reduction removes the water from a mix of ingredients to create a more concentrated flavor. For instance, a red wine reduction is red wine simmered to reduce by half.

ROUX

A good roux adds flavor while thickening the soup or sauce. Here is an in depth look at roux and its many variations.

There are four varieties of roux: white, cooked for the shortest time; blond, brown, and dark brown, which cooks the longest.

White and blond roux are commonly used to thicken sauces, soups and chowders. Brown and dark brown roux have more flavor, but less thickening power than white or blond roux.

Cook and store a batch of roux for future use. If you use butter and make roux balls, or buerre manie, it will harden in the fridge and make a smooth soup.

Roux takes mere minutes to make. Whether big or small batches, the proportions are the same, by weight: ***1 part oil or fat and 1 part all-purpose flour.***

Roux - Small Batch

Heat 2 tablespoons oil or fat in a saucepan over medium heat until it sizzles. Whisk in 3½ tablespoons of flour and whisk gently to form a thick paste. Keep whisking as the roux bubbles and cooks to the shade desired. Do not allow it to bubble too vigorously, you don't want *buerre noir*.

White Roux loses its raw smell after about 5 minutes and is slightly grainy in texture. The color is really *off white*.

Blond Roux smells like popcorn after about 20 minutes. It is tan, smooth, thinner than the white roux.

Brown Roux takes up to 35 minutes of cooking and stirring, and is a caramel brown color with a sharp nutty flavor.

Dark Brown Roux is cooked and stirred for 45 minutes and will look and smell like chocolate. This roux is thinner than the others.

Choose the right roux for your intended flavor.

Adding Liquid to Roux

After cooking roux, adding a liquid ingredient will make a sauce (and adding a lot more liquid, makes a soup.)

For lump-free thickening when making sauces, the liquid ingredient should be cold or room temperature, slowly whisked into the hot roux. Add the liquid a little at a time, whisking between each addition until the roux forms a paste, then whisking in the remaining liquid and bringing the mixture to a simmer. Cold or room temperature roux is whisked into a simmering soup or sauce until it dissolves.

Roux in soup or sauce should be simmered up to 20 minutes to reach full flavor and thickening potential and allows the flour to soften and absorb the liquid, which makes for a very smooth soup or sauce.

Protein & Vegetable Combinations

	Beef	Pork	Lamb	Poultry	Seafood	Veg
Arugula	X	X		X	X	X
Asparagus	X	X		X	X	X
Beets	X	X				
Broccoli	X	X		X		
Br Sprouts	X	X	X	X		X
Cabbage	X	X		X		
Carrots	X	X	X	X		X
Cauliflower		X		X		X
Chard	X			X		X
Celery	X	X	X	X	X	X
Corn	X			X		
Cucumber		X		X	X	X
Ginger	X	X			X	X
Jicama				X	X	
Leeks	X	X	X			

	Beef	Pork	Lamb	Poultry	Seafood	Veg
Mushrooms	X			X		X
Onions	X	X	X	X		X
Parsnips				X		
Peppers	X	X	X	X		X
Potatoes	X	X	X	X		X
Scallions	X	X	X	X	X	X
Shallots	X	X	X	X		X
Spinach		X		X		
Squash (summer)			X		X	
Squash (winter)	X	X		X		X
Sweet Potatoes	X	X	X	X		X
Tomatoes	X	X	X	X	X	X
Zucchini		X		X		

The Basic Soup Kit & Plan

Here is everything you need, and the order in which you need to use it, to make a good soup from scratch.

The Pot:

Heavy bottomed, non-reactive, stainless steel—not aluminum. Large.

The Fat:

Ghee, butter, olive oil or sunflower oil, bacon, chicken. If no fat required, use a small amount of stock.

Seeds and spices:

For Indian or Asian soups, pop seeds and bloom spices (mustard, fenugreek, cinnamon, cardamom, coriander, cumin, etc.) in hot fat before next step. Spices can be coarsely ground with mortar and pestle if desired.

Protein:

If including protein, such as chicken of beef, sauté it in the fat, remove from pan, and then sauté the veggies or Mirepoix in the combined fat.

Mirepoix:

The holy trinity of French cooking: carrots, onions, celery and perhaps garlic.

When "sweating" the Mirepoix, be careful not to let it brown—that would be caramelized. Size of veggies effects cooking time. Large chunks may be used for a soup that is to be pureed.

Herbs:

Add fresh or dried herbs now. Use the woody, hard herbs here, like rosemary, bay, thyme or sage.

Liquid:

Add more liquid than you think you need—it reduces in volume during cooking. Use rich stock, white wine, and/or liquid from other cooked veggies or potatoes.

Vegetables:

Add lighter vegetables, such as zucchini, summer squash, tomatoes or mushrooms.

Thickener:

For blended or thick soup, baked bread pieces, cooked rice, mashed potatoes, cornstarch or a roux may be added here. Soup may now be puréed, by cooling and placing in food processor in batches or with a immersion soup-blender.

Final Vegetables:

Add quick cooking vegetables last (peas, broccoli, spinach).

Beans, rice or starchy vegetables:

For a thick or substantial soup, add beans, potatoes, rice or lentils. (Pre-cook the beans or rice or lentils separately and add them at the end with the final vegetables so the beans, rice or lentils don't soak up all of your stock).

Herbs and spices:

Tender herbs (tarragon, basil, chives, parsley, chervil) can be added now to retain flavor and freshness. Also, for Asian or Indian soup, additional ground spices may be added now (curry, five spice powder).

Dairy or other flavors:

Unsalted butter, milk, cream, aioli, pesto, coconut milk, yogurt. Heat through, garnish and serve.

Garnish:

Add croutons, sour cream, fresh herbs in tureen or serving bowls. Make sure bowls are pre-warmed to retain heat.

Presentation:

Beautiful.

On the following page: Carrot Ginger Bisque

Chicken Stocks and Soups

First You Roast the Chicken

Roasting a chicken is a primary cooking skill. Recently, I heard David describe to a friend *Roasted Chicken à la GB*.

He said, "First you roast the chicken, then you save the 'jelly.'" [In my kitchen, this is the poaching liquid left in the pan.] "You have warm roasted chicken for dinner with something to pour the juices and the jelly over (saving some for soup, of course). The next day Ginna *pulls* the rest of the meat from the bird and you have chicken salad for lunch. The stock burbles all day. The next day there is soup, and the rest of the stock goes into the fridge. Somewhere along the line there is creamy chicken something with rice or mushrooms. Ginna gets a lot out of a 4 pound chicken."

Roasted Chicken à la GB

Serves 4–6

One Whole Roasting Chicken, about 4 pounds
Olive Oil
Salt
Herbs, optional
Juice and wine
Lemon or onion or both

Rinse a fat chicken thoroughly in cold water. Brined chickens are particularly nice, but hard to find.

Pat dry and let stand at room temperature for about an hour to dry out the skin.

Pre-heat oven to 350°

Place dry, room temperature chicken in a sprayed or oiled ceramic roasting pan (not glass - it splatters grease all over the place) and drizzle with olive oil. Rub it into the skin with your fingers. Rinse your fingers.

Sprinkle chicken with salt and herbs (unless it is a brined chicken - then skip the salt).

Pour ½ cup orange or apple or grape or pomegranate juice (with or without the wine) into the roasting pan and stick a washed lemon and/or a whole unpeeled onion (with the ends cut off) into the cavity.

Cover the chicken with a foil tent (spray the inside of the foil tent so it won't stick to the chicken skin).

Poach for one hour.

Remove the foil tent and baste the chicken every 30 minutes for another two hours.

The chicken will get browned and crusty. Lots of basting liquid develops.

When you remove the chicken from the oven, pour off the juices/jelly into a bowl to refrigerste for later use in the soup you created from the stock you made from the chicken you roasted.

For an easy **Roasted Chicken Stock**, pull the meat from the bones. Fill a one gallon pot with water and place in it the bones. Simmer for eight hours, adding water periodically to keep the level at one gallon. Strain into jars when cooled.

Clear Chicken Stock

Makes about one gallon

1 chicken, plucked and washed

2 carrots, cut in large chunks

3 celery stalks, cut in large chunks

2 large white onions, quartered

1 head of garlic, halved

1 each: rutabaga, parsnip, turnip, halved

2 bay leaves

1 teaspoon salt

3 quarts water

Brush and clean the vegetables and place in a large stockpot over medium heat. Add about 4 quarts water.

Gently place whole chicken in the pot.

Toss in the bay leaves and salt and allow it to slowly come to a simmer.

Lower the heat to medium low and gently simmer for 2 hours, partially covered.

Carefully strain the stock through a fine sieve into another pot to remove the vegetable solids. Cool.

It's best to refrigerate the stock overnight to make it easier to skim the fat, but the stock can be used immediately. Use the chicken meat in a finished soup, casserole or curry.

Refrigerate for up to two weeks or freeze.

Dark Chicken Stock

Makes about one gallon

1 lb legs, backs and wings of chicken

olive oil, salt and fresh or dried herbs

2 carrots, cut in large chunks

3 celery stalks, cut in large chunks

2 large white onions, quartered

1 head of garlic, halved

1 each rutabaga, parsnip, turnip, halved

Dried herbs

2 bay leaves

1 teaspoon salt

4 quarts water

Cover two half sheet pans with parchment. Place chicken pieces on one, the vegetables on the other. Coat with olive oil, salt and herbs. Roast in 350° oven for about an hour.

Remove from oven and cool to a handling point.

Place roasted chicken pieces and vegetables in a large stockpot over medium heat. Add about 4 quarts water. Toss in the bay leaves and salt and allow it to slowly come to a simmer.

Turn the heat to medium low and gently simmer for 3 hours, partially covered.

Be careful not to boil the stock. This causes the protein bits to separate and cloud an otherwise beautiful stock.

Remove from heat and cool slightly before the next step.

Carefully strain the stock through a fine sieve into another pot to remove the solids. Use the stock immediately or refrigerate for up to two weeks or freeze.

Other Uses for Chicken Stock

Sauces: Many sauces begin with a deeply flavored base—usually stock.

Curries: The word "curry" in Sanskrit simply means "sauce." In traditional East Indian or Asian cooking, there is no such thing as curry powder. A curry can be just about anything: yellow, brown, green, red. In making any kind of curry, a good stock is the best base. *See page 174 for Curry info.*

Cooking liquid: Use stock as the liquid for cooking rice or other grains.

Stock Cubes: Pour cooled stock into dedicated ice cube trays and freeze overnight. Remove Stock Cubes and place in a dedicated freezer bag and store in freezer for future use. Can be added to rice water, sauce, or simply enjoyed hot in a cup.

Bread liquid: Cooled stock will add flavor to bread, too.

Tips:

Do not boil stock—boiling separates the proteins and makes the stock cloudy.

Simmer Fish and Vegetable Stocks for 30 minutes max.

To make bone broth, simmer a pot full of roasted chicken bones for up to eight hours to extract all the collagen and flavor. Cool and strain. Store in glass jars in fridge. Lasts up to two weeks. Can be frozen in plastic or ice cube trays, see above.

Remove fat from stock that has been refrigerated overnight by just skimming it off the top.

Reserve the jelly in its own glass or ceramic bowl and refrigerate overnight. Skim the fat off the top with a spoon. Add the jelly to soups and sauces for even deeper flavor.

Save your salt for the end result. In other words, don't salt the stock, just the soup.

Soup of Consolation

In my novel series, *Lavandula* (including *Looking for John Steinbeck, Deke Interrupted* and their continuing sequels—at the time of this writing still in creation), Fáno sooths the family angst with *Soup of Consolation*. It is his answer to everything from the common cold to tears, tummy upsets to tummy butterflies.

Fáno's not-so-secret recipe is found only in *The Soup Kit*.

Makes about 2 gallons

Roasted Chicken, *see page 46*

10 cups assorted vegetables, rough cut: carrots, celery, onions, garlic, potatoes, yams

3 tablespoons butter

2 cloves garlic

8 cups Roasted Chicken Stock, *see page 49–52*

Pinch each: tarragon, oregano, thyme

Salt and pepper to taste

Herbs of love, spice of affection

    In a large soup or stock pot, sauté vegetables in butter and garlic.

    Add one cup of the stock.

    Using hand blender, grind vegetables with stock to make a smooth paste.

    Slowly add the rest of the stock and herbs.

    Simmer about fifteen minutes.

    Serve warm with finely shredded chicken and Star Croutons.

Star Croutons

Preheat oven to 200°

Six pieces stale bread—white or wheat
Olive oil
Mixed herbs such as Tarragon, Thyme, Oregano
Small star cutters

    Using star cutters, make about two cups star-shaped croutons.

    Spread on sheet pan.

    Drizzle with olive oil and sprinkle with herb mixture.

    Bake at 200° for about ten minutes, until crispy but not browned.

    Don't over-bake. When cooled, preserve in zip lock baggie until used.

Chicken Noodle

Makes more than two gallons

2½ pounds bone-in, skin-on chicken thighs

¼ teaspoon pepper
½ teaspoon salt
1 tablespoon sunflower oil

1 large onion, chopped
1 garlic clove, minced
4 celery ribs, chopped
4 medium carrots, chopped

10 cups Clear Chicken Stock, *see page 49*

2 bay leaves
1 teaspoon minced fresh thyme or ¼ teaspoon dried thyme
1 tablespoon chopped fresh parsley
1 tablespoon lemon juice
2 cups chopped tomatoes
3 cups cooked and cooled egg noodles

Pat chicken dry with paper towels; sprinkle with ½ teaspoon pepper and salt.

In a stockpot, heat oil over medium-high heat.

Add chicken, skin side down; cook until dark golden brown, 3–4 minutes.

Remove chicken from pan; remove and discard skin from chicken.

Reserve some pan drippings.

Add onion to drippings; cook and stir over medium-high until tender, 5 minutes.

Add garlic; cook 1 minute.

Add stock, loosening browned bits in pan with spoon or spatula.

Bring to a simmer.

Return chicken to pan. Add celery, carrots, bay leaves and thyme.

Simmer, covered, until chicken is tender, 25–30 minutes.

Transfer chicken to a plate and when cooled enough to handle, remove and discard the bones.

Remove soup from heat.

Shred meat into bite-sized pieces and return to stockpot.

Stir in parsley and lemon juice. Adjust seasoning with salt and pepper.

Discard bay leaves.

Serve over cooked noodles and chopped tomatoes.

Asparagus

Serves 4–6

2 pounds fresh asparagus

1 large onion, chopped

3 tablespoons unsalted butter

5 cups chicken stock

½ cup crème fraîche or heavy cream

lemon juice

Cut tips from the asparagus 1½ inches from top and halve tips lengthwise if thick. Reserve.

Cut remaining asparagus into ½-inch pieces.

Cook onion in 2 tablespoons butter in your soup pot over moderately low heat, stirring, until soft.

Add asparagus and salt and pepper to taste. Cook, stirring, 5 minutes.

Add chicken stock and simmer until asparagus is tender, about 15 minutes.

Roast reserved asparagus tips by laying on a parchment covered sheet pan, sprinkle with olive oil and salt. Roast about 20 minutes.

Purée soup with immersion blender until smooth. Stir in crème fraiche.

Add more stock to thin soup if necessary.

Season with salt and pepper.

Bring soup to a boil and whisk in remaining tablespoon butter.

Add lemon juice and garnish with asparagus tips.

Pour into warm bowls and serve.

Minestrone

Serves 6–8

2 tablespoons extra-virgin olive oil

1 large onion, diced

4 cloves garlic, minced

2 stalks celery, diced

1 large carrot, diced

⅓ pound green beans, trimmed and cut into ½-inch pieces (about 1½ cups)

1 teaspoon dried oregano

1 teaspoon dried basil

Kosher salt and freshly ground pepper

3 cups chopped Roma tomatoes

6 cups Chicken Stock, *pages 49–52*

1 cup cooked kidney beans

1 cup cooked elbow pasta

⅓ cup finely grated Parmesan cheese

2 tablespoons chopped fresh basil

Heat the olive oil in a large pot over medium-high heat. Add the onion and cook until translucent, about 4 minutes. Add the garlic and cook 30 seconds.

Add the celery and carrot and cook until they begin to soften, about 5 minutes.

Stir in the green beans, dried oregano and basil, ¾ teaspoon salt, and pepper to taste; cook 3 more minutes.

Add the tomatoes and chicken stock to the pot and bring to a simmer. Reduce the heat to medium low and simmer 10 minutes.

Stir in the kidney beans and pasta and heat through.

Season with salt. Ladle into bowls and top with the Parmesan and chopped basil.

Chicken Chowder

Serves 6–8

1 lb chopped bacon
1 cup fresh or frozen corn
1 medium onion
2 carrots
3 stalks celery
6–8 Yukon Gold potatoes
2 cloves garlic
6 cups chicken stock
1 teaspoon chopped fresh or dry tarragon
salt and pepper to taste

2 cups cooked chicken

Preheat oven to 350°

Place bacon in a soup pot and fry until crispy.

Thaw corn if frozen and sauté in the bacon fat. Remove corn from pan and set aside.

Sauté onion, carrots and celery in remaining bacon fat. Add oil if necessary.

Add potatoes and garlic and simmer for about 5 minutes.

Add chicken stock, salt, pepper and tarragon and simmer 30 minutes.

Add sautéed corn and cooked chicken.

Serve warm.

Thai Coconut

Serves 2–4

1 tablespoon vegetable oil

10 prawns/shrimp, peeled and deveined

2 garlic cloves, finely grated

2 teaspoon ginger, finely grated

1 stalk lemongrass, peeled, finely grated

1 tablespoon brown sugar

1½ tablespoon fish sauce (or soy sauce)

2 teaspoon yellow curry powder

1 teaspoon coriander powder

2 teaspoon chili paste

14 oz can coconut milk

2 cups Chicken or Vegetable Stock, *pages 49–52 or 96*

2 teaspoon lime zest (1 lime)

7 oz fresh egg noodles, cooked according to directions

Big handful of bean sprouts

Serve with:

Lime wedges

Fresh cilantro

Sliced red or green onion

Fried shallots

Heat oil in a large saucepan over high heat. Add prawns and sear both sides until light golden. Set aside.

Turn heat to medium. If pot is dry add a touch of oil.

Add garlic, ginger and lemongrass. Sauté until garlic is golden, about 20 seconds.

Add sugar and fish sauce. Stir and cook until it looks like caramel, less than a minute.

Add chili paste, cilantro and yellow curry powder. Stir and cook for 30 seconds.

Add chicken broth and coconut milk. Stir and bring to simmer. Simmer for 2 minutes, then add lime zest and return prawns into broth.

Cook for 2 minutes to reheat and cook the prawns.

Ladle soup over the cooked noodles in the bowl.

Add toppings of choice and a squeeze of lime juice.

Avgolemono

Serves 4–6

4 cups Chicken Stock, *pages 49–52*

Salt and freshly ground pepper

2 cups cooked white rice, warmed

2 large egg yolks

¼ cup plus 2 tablespoons fresh lemon juice

1 roasted chicken, meat pulled from the bones and coarsely shredded (1 pound)

¼ cup chopped fresh dill

In a large saucepan, season the stock with salt and pepper and bring to a simmer.

To 1 cup of the hot stock add ½ cup of the rice, the egg yolks and the lemon juice and purée with immersion blender until smooth.

Stir the purée into the simmering stock along with the cooked chicken and remaining 1½ cups of rice.

Simmer until thickened slightly, 10 minutes. Stir in the dill and serve.

Egg Drop

Serve 6-8

4 cups Chicken Stock, divided, *pages 49–52*

⅛ teaspoon ground ginger

2 tablespoons chopped fresh chives

1½ tablespoons cornstarch

2 eggs

1 egg yolk

Reserve ¾ cup of chicken broth, pour the rest into a soup pan.

Stir the salt, ginger and chives into the saucepan, and bring to a rolling boil.

In a cup or small bowl stir together the remaining stock and cornstarch until smooth. Set aside.

In a small bowl, whisk the eggs and egg yolk with a fork.

Drizzle a little egg at a time from the fork into the boiling stock mixture. Eggs will cook immediately.

Once the eggs have been dropped, gradually stir in the cornstarch mixture until the soup is the desired consistency.

Serve immediately.

Hot & Sour

Serves 6–8

1 block firm tofu
2 ounces cooked pork tenderloin
Marinade:
1 teaspoon soy sauce
½ teaspoon sesame oil
1 teaspoon or cornstarch

½ cup bamboo shoots
2 tablespoons black fungus (Wood Ear)
or Cloud Ear fungus*
(or 3–4 Chinese dried black mushrooms
or fresh mushrooms)*
1 small handful dried lily buds*

6 cups Chicken Stock, *pages 49–52*
1 teaspoon salt, or to taste
1 teaspoon granulated sugar
2 tablespoons soy sauce
2 tablespoons rice vinegar
1 tablespoon cornstarch
dissolved in ¼ cup water
1 egg, beaten
1 green onion, finely chopped
white pepper to taste
hot chili oil, to taste, optional

Ingredients with a * are the hard-to-find things, not in most supermarkets.

Shred pork.

Mix marinade ingredients and marinate pork for 20 minutes.

Cut tofu into bite-sized cubes.

Cut bamboo shoots into thin, fine slices.

Soak fungus in warm water for 20 minutes. Rinse, and cut into thin pieces.

(If using Chinese dried mushrooms, soak, then cut off the stems and cut them into thin strips. If using fresh mushrooms, just brush and slice.)

Bring the stock to a simmer. Add bamboo shoots, fungus or mushrooms, and the lily buds, if you have them.

(You can make a more Americanized version without these things, because you might drive all over town to find lily buds!)

Stir. Add tofu.

Simmer and add the marinated pork.

Stir in the salt, sugar, soy sauce and vinegar and sesame oil.

Mix the cornstarch with water.

While stirring, slowly add the cornstarch mixture to the soup.

Bring back to a simmer and remove from heat.

Slowly drop in the beaten egg, stirring in one direction.

Add the green onion and the white pepper to taste.

Serve with chili oil.

(**Hot and Sour Soup** can be frozen without the tofu. Add it when thawed and reheating for serving.)

Wonton

Wontons:
1 cup cooked shrimp, chopped
1 green onion
2 tablespoons cilantro, chopped
2 tablespoons Chinese Rice Wine
1 tablespoon soy sauce
bowl of water
1 package egg roll wrappers

Combine cooked shrimp (or pork or ground turkey), onions and cilantro with wine and soy sauce and set aside for ten minutes. Form into balls and place in center of egg roll wrapper. Fold over or pinch together, gluing the edges with water.

Soup:
3 tablespoons peanut oil
2 chicken breasts, cut bite size
1 pound shrimp, cleaned and deveined
1 can water chestnuts, sliced
1 bunch scallions, sliced
1 pound shitake mushrooms, sliced
2 carrots, sliced
1 stalk celery, sliced
2 cloves garlic, minced
4 cups Chicken Stock, *pages 49-52*

Sauté chicken pieces, then shrimp in hot oil and remove from pot. Add new oil and sauté vegetables. Remove from pot. Add chicken stock to pot bring to simmer. Add wontons and cook for five minutes. Add cooked vegetables, chicken and shrimp. Garnish with scallions or cilantro. Serve hot.

Albondigas

Serves 4–6

1 pound ground beef
1 egg, beaten
minced garlic
chopped cilantro
cumin, salt & pepper to taste
cooked rice (optional)

4 cups Chicken Stock, *pages 49–52*
½ carrot sliced
1 celery stalk cut into chunks
2 cups diced tomatoes
½ teaspoon ground cumin
1 teaspoon oregano
½ cup cilantro
1 potato diced
salt and pepper to taste

Meatballs: Combine first six ingredients thoroughly. Form 20–24 tight meatballs by rolling between your palms. Brown in a hot pan for a few minutes on each side. Set aside.

Soup: In a large pot, combine chicken stock, carrots, celery, tomatoes, cumin, oregano, and cilantro leaves. Bring to a boil, and reduce heat to a mild simmer for 10 minutes.

Drop meatballs and potatoes in the soup. Return to simmer and cook another 20 minutes.

Salt and Pepper to taste. Enjoy warm.

Tortilla

Serves 4–6

vegetable or corn oil

2 cups fresh or frozen corn, thawed, patted dry
    and pan-roasted in

1 tablespoon butter

1 teaspoon ground cumin

1 medium yellow onion, chopped

3 carrots, chopped

3 stalks celery, chopped

3 cloves garlic, chopped

1 to 2 chipotle peppers

2 cups diced tomatoes

½ cup tomato sauce

salt and pepper

3 cups Chicken or Veggie Stock, *pages 49–52 or 96*

1 cup shredded Cheddar cheese

½ cup sour cream

3 cups tortilla chips, broken into pieces

Heat two tablespoons oil in a large soup pot. Add cumin, onions, carrots, celery, garlic and chipotle peppers. Cook 5 minutes.

Add tomatoes, tomato sauce and 1 ½ cups stock. Blend with immersion blender.

Add remaining stock and simmer. Add pan-roasted corn.

Serve soup with shredded cheese and sour cream. Top with tortilla pieces.

Chicken Sausage Stew

Serves 4-6

1 tablespoon extra virgin olive oil

8 ounces boneless skinless chicken breast, cut into ½ inch pieces

1 (10 ounce) package Italian sausage, cooked and cut into ½ inch pieces

1 medium onion, chopped

2 cups diced carrots

2 cups diced celery

1 large garlic cloves, thinly sliced

1 teaspoon fennel seeds

6 cups diced Roma tomatoes

1 cup chopped fresh parsley

4 cups Chicken Stock , *pages 49–52*

1 cup rotini pasta, cooked and drained

Salt and black pepper to taste

½ cup grated Parmesan cheese

2 tablespoons chopped fresh basil

Heat a 4-quart stock pot on medium heat. Add olive oil and brown the chicken pieces. Remove chicken and set aside. Return the pan to the heat and add the sausage. Brown evenly.

Add the onion, carrot, celery, garlic and fennel seed and stir. Simmer 7 to 8 minutes.

Add diced tomatoes, parsley, and chicken stock. Return chicken and sausage to pot. Bring to boil and cover. Reduce heat to simmer and cook until carrots are tender, about 5 minutes. Add the pasta. Turn off the heat and let the soup rest for 5 minutes. Season with salt and black pepper. Transfer to serving bowl and sprinkle with Parmesan cheese and basil.

Chicken Chili

Serves 10–12

1 Roasted Chicken, *see page 46*

2 cups chopped onion

4 garlic cloves, chopped

1½ tablespoons cumin seeds

¼ cup olive oil

4 cups fresh Roma tomatoes

2 cups fresh Enchilada Sauce, *see page 173*

¼ cup chili powder

1 tablespoon dried hot red pepper flakes

1 teaspoon dried oregano

½ teaspoon cinnamon

1 oz baker's chocolate

1 tablespoon salt

½ teaspoon black pepper

4 cups cooks red beans

sour cream

coarsely grated cheddar

In a large heavy pot cook the onion and the garlic and cumin seeds in the oil over moderate heat, stirring, until golden.

Add tomatoes and Enchilada Sauce, the chili powder, red pepper flakes, oregano, cinnamon, chocolate, salt, and pepper, and stir.

Simmer uncovered, stirring occasionally, for 2 hours, or until thickened.

Stir the cooked red beans into the chili and simmer, stirring occasionally, for 10 minutes.

Add Roasted chicken.

The chili may be made in advance.

Cool uncovered, then keep covered and chilled for 2 days or covered and frozen for 2 months.

Serve the chili topped with the sour cream and cheddar.

Tom Kha Gai

Made with coconut milk, galangal, lemon grass and chicken. The fried chilies add a smoky flavor as well as texture, color and heat, but not so much that it overwhelms the soup.

Serves 4–6

1 pound boneless skinless chicken breasts

3 tablespoons vegetable oil

2 (14 oz) cans coconut milk

2 cups Chicken Stock, *pages 49–52*

1 cup white mushrooms, sliced

1 (1 inch) piece ginger, peeled and halved

3 tablespoons fish sauce

¼ cup freshly squeezed lime juice

¼ teaspoon cayenne pepper or more to taste

2 stalks fresh lemongrass, tough outer layers removed, cut into 4 pieces

thinly sliced green onion for garnish

chopped fresh cilantro for garnish

Cut chicken into chunks. Heat pan over medium heat. Add in oil and chicken and sauté 2 to 3 minutes. Salt slightly. The chicken won't be cooked through, but will continue to cook in the soup later.

In the soup pot, bring coconut milk and chicken stock to a simmer over medium heat. Whisk to break up coconut milk.

Add chicken, mushrooms, ginger, fish sauce, lime juice, cayenne powder and lemon grass. Simmer until the chicken is done and the mushrooms are tender, 10 to 15 minutes.

Sprinkle with green onion and fresh cilantro and serve steaming hot.

Mulligatawny

(from the Tamil word meaning 'pepper water')

Serves 4-6

½ cup chopped onion

2 stalks celery, chopped

1 carrot, diced

¼ cup butter

1½ tablespoons all-purpose flour

1½ teaspoons curry powder, *see page 174*

4 cups Chicken Stock, *pages 49-52*

½ apple, cored and chopped

¼ cup white rice

1 skinless, boneless chicken breast half, cut into cubes

salt to taste

ground black pepper to taste

1 pinch dried thyme

½ cup heavy cream, heated

Sauté onions, celery, carrot, and butter in a large soup pot.

Add flour and curry, and cook 5 more minutes.

Add chicken stock, mix well, and bring to a boil. Simmer about ½ hour.

Add apple, rice, chicken, salt, pepper, and thyme. Simmer 15-20 minutes, or until rice is done.

Serve with hot cream.

Roasted Potato Leek

Serves 4–6

2 teaspoons ghee

8 medium potatoes, quartered

2 large leeks, washed and chopped and washed again

3 carrots, large cuts

2 stalks celery, large cuts

1 clove garlic,

4 cups Chicken Stock, *pages 49–52*

1 teaspoon salt

1 teaspoon tarragon

¼ teaspoon thyme

pinch of fresh grated nutmeg

1 pint plain yogurt or sour cream

Drizzle olive oil and sprinkle salt on the potatoes, carrots, celery, leeks, garlic and roast in a 350° oven for 30 minutes or until caramelized.

Heat the ghee in a large soup pot. Add mustard and cumin seeds and stir until they begin to pop.

Add the potatoes, carrots, celery, leeks, garlic and stir. Sauté until translucent.

Slowly add 2 or 3 cups stock. Blend well. Using an immersion blender or food processor, blend until smooth.

Add more stock for desired consistency.

Add herbs. Salt to taste.

Serve with dollops of yogurt or sour cream (thin the yogurt or sour cream with water or milk if it is heavier than your soup) and a sprinkling of nutmeg.

Seafood Stocks and Soups

Seafood Stock (Fumé)

Fish Stock is quick and easy to make, and is a magnificent base for fish soups, chowders, seafood risotto, any number of sauces.

The best fish bones to use are those from mild, lean, white fish like halibut, cod or flounder. Fish to avoid are salmon, trout, mackerel or other oily, fatty fish. Lobster and shrimp shells work well, too.

Makes 1 gallon

4 lbs fish bones (or shells)
1 gallon water
1 cup white wine
1 stalk celery, chopped
1 carrot, peeled and chopped
1 yellow onion, peeled and chopped
2 tablespoons butter

Sachet

2–3 whole peppercorns
3–4 parsley stems
1 bay leaf
1 whole clove
1 pinch dried thyme

Make the sachet by tying the thyme, peppercorns, clove, parsley stems and bay leaf into a piece of cheesecloth.

In a heavy-bottomed stock pot or soup pot, heat the butter over medium heat. Lower the heat, add the vegetables and sweat, with the lid on, for about 5 minutes or until the onions are softened and slightly translucent.

Don't brown the vegetables.

Add the fish bones and sweat for another couple of minutes, covered, until the bones are slightly opaque.

Add the wine and bring up the heat until it starts to simmer.

Then add the sachet and let simmer for 30 minutes.

Strain (remove fish bones first if that makes it easier), cool and refrigerate.

A Quick Fish Stock

For an emergency...

Makes about 2.5 cups

1 cup water
1 cup dry vermouth
1 cup bottled clam juice
2 diced celery ribs
1 small diced onion
3 springs parsley

Combine all ingredients and simmer until reduced two about 2.5 cups.

Strain and season.

Lobster Bisque

Serves 4-6

One lobster tail

Water

Lemongrass

1 tablespoon butter

2 carrots, peeled and chopped

2 stalks celery, chopped

three shallots, chopped

1 tablespoon butter mixed with one tablespoon olive oil

pinches of tarragon and thyme

3 tablespoons flour/3 tablespoons butter

3 Roma tomatoes, cut in pieces or two tablespoons tomato purée.

Place 6 cups water in a large pot. Wash lobster tail and put in simmering water with lemongrass, salt and pepper. Simmer ten minutes.

Remove lobster tail, cool and shell it.

Place shell back into stock pot. Simmer 30 minutes for a rich fish stock. Set aside.

Gently slice lobster and sauté in butter. Set Aside.

Sauté Mirepoix (carrots, celery, shallots) in butter/olive oil mixture. Add a little more butter, if necessary, and the flour. Blend with spoon to make a roux.

Add tomatoes and herbs. Slowly add the fish stock, stirring constantly. Simmer until thickened. You may add chicken stock for a richer flavor.

Purée with immersion blender until smooth. Set aside until ready to serve.

Divide the lobster meat among the serving bowls.

Pour lobster bisque into bowls. Serve with crème fraiche and chives.

Cioppino

Serves 6–8

3 tablespoons olive oil

1 large fennel bulb, thinly sliced

1 onion, chopped

3 large shallots, chopped

2 teaspoons salt

4 large garlic cloves, finely chopped

¾ teaspoon dried crushed red pepper flakes, plus more to taste

¼ cup tomato paste

3 cups fresh tomatoes, chopped

1½ cups dry white wine

5 cups Fish Stock, *page 82*

1 bay leaf

1 pound manila clams, scrubbed

1 pound mussels, scrubbed, de-bearded

1 pound uncooked large shrimp, peeled and deveined

1½ pounds assorted firm-fleshed fish fillets such as halibut or salmon, cut into 2-inch chunks

Heat the oil in a very large pot over medium heat. Add the fennel, onion, shallots, and salt and sauté until the onion is translucent, about 10 minutes.

Add the garlic and ¾ teaspoon of red pepper flakes, and sauté 2 minutes.

Stir in the tomato paste. Add tomatoes with their juices, wine, fish stock and bay leaf.

Cover and bring to a simmer. Reduce the heat to medium-low.

Simmer covered until the flavors blend, about 30 minutes.

Add clams and mussels. Cover and cook until clams and mussels begin to open, about 5 minutes.

Add the shrimp and fish. Simmer gently until the fish and shrimp are just cooked through, and the clams are completely open, stirring gently, about 5 minutes longer (discard any clams and mussels that do not open).

Season the soup, to taste, with more salt and red pepper flakes.

Ladle the soup into bowls and serve.

Bouillabaisse

Serves 6–8

2 lobster tails

2 large tomatoes, peeled and chopped

1 large onion, chopped

4 garlic cloves, chopped

½ cup extra-virgin olive oil

1 lb boiling potatoes

⅓ cup finely chopped fennel fronds (sometimes called anise)

1 bay leaf

¼ teaspoon crumbled saffron threads

1½ tablespoons coarse sea salt

½ teaspoon black pepper

9 cups Fish Stock, *page 82*

3 pounds white fish fillets (such as turbot, red snapper, striped bass and/or cod), cut into 2-inch pieces

½ pound small hard-shelled clams, scrubbed

½ pound cultivated mussels, scrubbed and any beards removed

½ pound large shrimp in shells

Put oven rack in middle position and preheat oven to 250°F.
Arrange bread slices in 1 layer in a shallow baking pan and brush both sides with oil. Bake until crisp, about 30 minutes. Rub 1 side of each toast with a cut side of garlic. Cook lobster in boiling water for two minutes. Transfer lobster with tongs to a colander and let stand until cool enough to handle. Discard hot water in pot. Put lobster in a shallow baking pan. Crack shells with a mallet or rolling pin. Cut crosswise through shell into 2-inch pieces. Reserve lobster juices that accumulate in baking pan.

Cook tomatoes, onion, and garlic in oil in cleaned 6- to 8-quart pot over moderate heat, stirring occasionally, until onion is softened, 5 to 7 minutes.

Meanwhile, peel potatoes and cut into ½-inch cubes. Stir potatoes into tomatoes with fennel fronds, bay leaf, saffron, sea salt, and pepper. Add stock and bring to a boil, then reduce heat and simmer, covered, until potatoes are almost tender, 8 to 10 minutes.

Add thicker pieces of fish and cockles to soup and simmer, covered, 2 minutes. Stir in mussels, shrimp, lobster, including juices, and remaining fish and simmer, covered, until they are just cooked through and mussels open wide, about 5 minutes.

Stir 3 tablespoons broth from soup into rouille until blended.

Arrange 2 croutons in each of 6 to 8 deep soup bowls. Carefully transfer fish and shellfish from soup to croutons with a slotted spoon, then ladle some broth with vegetables over seafood.

Top each serving with 1 teaspoon *rouille* and serve remainder on the side.

Rouille

3 tablespoons water

¾ cup coarse fresh bread crumbs (baguette, crust removed)

3 garlic cloves

½ teaspoon coarse sea salt

½ teaspoon cayenne

3 tablespoons extra-virgin olive oil

Pour water over bread crumbs in a bowl. Mash garlic to a paste with sea salt and cayenne using a mortar and pestle.

Add moistened bread crumbs and mash into garlic paste.

Add oil in a slow stream, mashing and stirring vigorously with pestle until combined well.

Clam Chowder

Serves 2–4

2 tablespoons unsalted butter
1 medium onion, finely diced
2 celery stalks sliced
3 tablespoons all-purpose flour
2 cups Chicken or Fish Stock, *pages 49–52 or 82*
2 (10-ounce) cans chopped clams in juice
1 cup heavy cream
2 bay leaves
1 pound Yukon gold potatoes, cubed
Salt and freshly ground black pepper

2 to 3 tablespoons unsalted butter
½ baguette, cut into 1-inch cubes
3 tablespoons freshly chopped flat-leaf parsley
Salt and freshly ground black pepper

Heat the butter in a large pot over medium-high heat. Add the onion and celery and sauté until softened, mixing often. Stir in the flour to distribute evenly. Add the stock, juice from 2 cans of chopped clams (reserve clams), cream, bay leaves, and potatoes and stir to combine. Bring to a simmer, stirring consistently (the mixture will thicken), then reduce the heat to medium-low and cook 20 minutes, stirring often, until the potatoes are nice and tender. Then add clams and season to taste with salt and pepper, cook until clams are just firm, another 2 minutes.

Croutons:

Melt the butter in a large skillet and toss the bread cubes in the butter until browned and toasted, about 2 to 3 minutes. Add parsley and season with salt and pepper.

On following page: Mushroom Bisque

Vegetable Stocks and Soups

Clear Vegetable Stock

Makes about one gallon

2 carrots, cut in large chunks

3 celery stalks, cut in large chunks

2 large white onions, quartered, skins on

1 head of garlic, halved

1 each rutabaga, parsnip, turnip, halved

2 bay leaves

1 teaspoon salt

4 quarts water

Brush and clean the vegetables and place in a large stockpot over medium heat.

Add about 4 quarts water.

Toss in the bay leaves and salt and allow it to slowly come to a simmer.

Turn the heat to medium-low and gently simmer for 3 hours, partially covered.

Carefully strain the stock through a fine sieve into another pot to remove the vegetable solids.

Use the stock immediately or if you plan to store it, place the pot in a sink full of ice water and stir to cool down the stock.

Cover and refrigerate for up to one week or freeze in containers.

Dark Vegetable Stock

Use this stock when a deep color and strong, smoky flavors will enhance the recipe. It can be kept for up to 5 days in the refrigerator, or frozen for up to 2 months.

Makes about one gallon

Preheat an oven to 400°F.

2 yellow onions, unpeeled, quartered
6 shallots
2 garlic cloves, unpeeled
1 carrot, peeled and cut in half
six stalks celery, cut in half
2 each parsnips, turnips, rutabagas
5–6 quarts water
salt and pepper
lemongrass stalk

> Place the vegetables on a sheet pan covered with parchment. Drizzle with olive oil, salt and pepper. Place in the oven and roast, turning the vegetables at least once during cooking, until the vegetables are well caramelized on some surfaces, about 55 minutes.
>
> Transfer the pan to the stove top and add water. Bring barely to a boil, then reduce the heat to low and simmer uncovered without allowing the water to bubble, for about 3 hours. The stock should be deeply colored and very aromatic.
>
> Strain through a fine-mesh sieve into containers. Let cool, cap tightly, and refrigerate or freeze.

Black Bean

Serves 6–8

6 cups cooked black beans

3 tablespoons olive oil or ghee

1 large yellow onion, chopped

3 stalks celery, chopped, with leaves

3 carrots, chopped

1 clove garlic, minced

1 bay leaf

10 cups Clear or Dark Veggie Stock, *see pages 96 & 97*

salt and pepper

6 hard boiled eggs, chopped

1 pint sour cream

2 bunches scallions, chopped

Sauté onions, celery, carrots and garlic in olive oil or ghee.

Add veggie stock. Bring to boil over medium high heat. Skim off rising foam.

Half cover the pot and reduce heat to low. Simmer for 30 minutes.

Remove bay leaf.

Blend soup in pot with handheld blender.

Heat through. If necessary, thin with stock.

Serve with hardboiled eggs, sour cream and scallions.

Heart Throb Café Bisque

named after a sweet but short-lived cafe in San Diego

Serves 6–8

10 cups assorted rough cut vegetables, including:

carrots, celery, onions, potatoes, yams

3 Tbsp clarified butter

2 cloves garlic

8 cups Dark Veggie Stock, *see page 96*

pinch each: Tarragon, Oregano, Thyme

salt and pepper to taste

herbs of love

spice of affection

In a large soup or stock pot, sauté vegetables in butter and garlic. Add one cup of the stock. Using hand blender, grind vegetables with stock to make a smooth paste. Slowly add the rest of the stock and herbs. Simmer about fifteen minutes. Serve warm with Star Croutons.

Star Croutons

Six pieces stale bread, white or wheat

Olive oil

Mixed herbs such as Tarragon, Thyme, Oregano

Small star cutters

Preheat oven to 200°

Using star cutters, make about two cups star-shaped croutons. Spread on sheet pan. Drizzle with olive oil and sprinkle with herb mixture.

Bake at 200° for about ten minutes, until crispy but not browned. Don't over-bake.

When cooled, preserve in zip lock baggie until used.

Pumpkin Bisque

Serves 6–8

3 sugar pie pumpkins, washed, cut in quarters or
2 quarts mashed pumpkin
3 tablespoons ghee
1 teaspoon brown mustard seeds
1 teaspoon cumin seeds
3 carrots, chopped
3 stalks celery, chopped
1 yellow onion, chopped
1 clove garlic, minced
2 inch piece ginger root, peeled and minced or crushed

1 tablespoon Thai-style chili paste
1 teaspoon cinnamon
½ teaspoon cloves
1 teaspoon kosher salt
4–5 cups Veggie Stock, *pages 96 or 97*
1 cup coconut milk
1 pint plain yogurt

Place pumpkin on a sheet pan lined with parchment. Bake at 350* for about 40 minutes, until cooked through and soft. Set aside.

When cooled, remove seeds and discard, scoop out pulp and place in a bowl.

Heat the ghee in a large pot. Add mustard and cumin seeds and stir until they begin to pop.

Add the carrots, celery, onion, garlic, ginger root, chili paste, cinnamon and cloves and stir.

Add the pumpkin mash and blend well.

Slowly add 2 or 3 cups stock. Blend well.

Using a handheld soup blender or food processor, process until smooth.

Add more stock to make desired consistency.

Add coconut milk to taste. Salt to taste.

Serve with dollops of yogurt (thin the yogurt with water or milk if it is heavier than your soup).

Butternut Squash

Serves 5–6

3 medium butternut squash,
    cut in large pieces, baked covered 45 minutes

½ teaspoon each: brown mustard seeds, cumin seeds, cardamom seeds

2 tablespoons ghee

¼ teaspoon salt

¼ teaspoon cinnamon

½ teaspoon grated fresh ginger

1 carrot, chopped

1 medium onion, chopped

1 stalk celery, chopped

1 clove garlic, minced

5 cups Veggie Stock, *pages 96 or 97*

½ can coconut milk

    Scoop pulp from squash.

    In soup pot, dry fry seeds for one minute.

    Add ghee.

    Add remaining spices and veggies. Sauté five minutes. Add Butternut pulp.

    Add stock. Simmer about 30 minutes.

    With hand held soup blender, mash pulp to blend with stock.

    Add coconut milk and bring to serving temp. Serve warm or chilled.

Beet & Watermelon Bisque with Orange and Ginger

Serves 6–8

2 pounds beets, scrubbed, quartered, rubbed with coconut oil and salted

2 tablespoons butter or coconut oil

2 cups chopped Mirepoix (carrots, onion, celery)

½ teaspoon ground ginger, or 1 one inch piece, minced

4–6 cups Clear Veggie Stock, *see page 96*

2 pounds watermelon, cut up and seeded, if necessary

1 quart orange juice

salt to taste

yogurt

grated nutmeg

mint sprigs

Roast beets at 350° for 45 minutes, until cooked through and caramelized.

Heat the butter or oil in a large pot. Sauté Mirepoix until translucent. Add beets and 2 or 3 cups stock. Simmer 20 minutes. Cool.

Add watermelon pieces. Using a handheld soup blender or food processor, process until smooth.

Add orange juice and a bit more veggie stock if necessary to smooth out flavors.

Salt to taste.

Serve at room temperature with dollops of yogurt or sour cream (thin the yogurt or sour cream with water or milk of it is heavier than your soup) and a sprinkling of nutmeg and a mint sprig.

Ginna BB Gordon

Chilled Cucumber

Serves 3-4

2 cucumbers
1¼ cups water
2 tablespoons ghee or butter
1 small onion
1 tablespoon flour
2½ cups Veggie Stock
¼ teaspoon ground cloves
10 tablespoon sour cream
1 tablespoon lemon juice
salt & pepper
chopped fresh mint

Peel and slice the cucumbers. Peel and finely chop onion.

Place the cucumbers and water in a saucepan and simmer until tender.

Purée the cucumbers and liquid in food processor.

In a larger saucepan, melt butter or ghee and "sweat" the onion until translucent, stir in the flour and mix well.

Gradually pour in the stock, stirring constantly until the mixture thickens.

Bring to a boil, turn to low and add the cucumber purée, cloves and lemon juice.

Season with salt & pepper. Simmer for two minutes.

Remove from heat and cool slightly. Strain through a fine sieve.

Cool completely. Stir in the sour cream.

Chill well before serving. Garnish with chopped mint.

Creamy Wild Mushroom

Serves 4–6

2 cups sherry

¼ cup butter, cubed

1 pound assorted fresh wild mushrooms (shiitake, crimini, lobster, oyster)

8 shallots, finely chopped

⅓ cup minced fresh parsley

1 tablespoon lemon juice

⅓ cup all-purpose flour

4 cups Dark Veggie or Dark Beef Broth, *pages 97 or 121*

8 ounces Brie, rind removed, cubed

1 cup heavy whipping cream

1 teaspoon salt

½ teaspoon white pepper

Place sherry in a small saucepan. Bring to a boil and reduce by half. Set aside.

Melt butter in a heavy-bottomed pot (like a Dutch oven). Add mushrooms and shallots and sauté until tender.

Add parsley and lemon juice. Stir in flour until blended; gradually add broth and reduced sherry.

Bring to a boil. Reduce heat and simmer uncovered for 8–10 minutes or until thickened. Stir in cheese and let it melt.

Add the cream, salt and pepper.

Heat through (do not boil) and serve.

Tomato

Serves 4–6

2½ pounds Plum or otherwise" meaty" tomatoes, coarsely chopped

3 cups Clear Veggie Stock, *page 96*

1 tablespoon tomato paste

1 onion, minced

2 garlic cloves, minced

1 teaspoon dried oregano

¼ teaspoon crushed red pepper

½ cup heavy cream

salt and freshly ground black pepper

In a medium saucepan, combine the tomatoes with the water, tomato paste, onion, garlic, oregano and crushed red pepper. Simmer over moderate heat, stirring a few times, until the tomatoes are very tender, about 20 minutes. Add the cream and simmer for 1 minute.

Purée the soup with immersion blender and pass it through a coarse strainer into a medium saucepan or pot. Season with salt and black pepper. Reheat and serve.

Broccoli Cheddar

Serves 6–8

½ cup butter

1 onion, chopped

2 cloves garlic, minced

2 tablespoons flour

½ teaspoon salt

2 cups broccoli flowerettes

6 cups Veggie Stock, *pages 96 or 97*

1 small block aged cheddar cheese, grated or cubed

1 cup heavy cream

In a stockpot, melt butter over medium heat. Cook onion in butter until softened.

Add garlic, cook another few minutes.

Sprinkle with flour and salt.

Stir in broccoli and cover with chicken stock.

Simmer until broccoli is tender, 10 to 15 minutes.

Cool for ten mintues then purée with immersion blender.

Return to heat and stir in cheese a little at a time until melted.

Mix in heavy cream. Reheat.

Serve warm.

Gazpacho

Tomatoes	Watermelon
Mango	Garlic
Cilantro	Red wine vinegar
Green peppers	Olive oil
Scallions	Salt
Cucumbers	Pepper

The tomatoes sold bagged at the end of the day at farmers' markets are ideal, but a mix of heirlooms would be perfect, too.

An easy rule of thumb is three parts tomatoes to one part other ingredients, such as red, yellow and green bell peppers, onions, garlic, scallions, peeled cucumbers and seedless watermelon, all cut into chunks. I sometimes add parsley, cilantro or any other leafy herbs that I have in the fridge.

Pack the vegetables in the blender, starting with the tomatoes because they're the juiciest. Add a good splash of red wine vinegar or sherry vinegar and a bigger splash of extra-virgin olive oil and season with salt and freshly ground pepper, then purée until chunky or smooth.

If you want to make a really thick gazpacho, soak a few pieces of country bread in water, squeeze dry and add them to the blender along with the vegetables.

Pour the gazpacho into a bowl and season the soup to taste with salt and pepper and additional vinegar and olive oil.

At this point, you can refrigerate it overnight.

Spinach Bisque

Serves 4–6

2 teaspoons ghee

2 large leeks, washed and chopped and washed again

3 carrots, chopped (if you like a greener soup, omit carrots)

2 stalks celery, chopped

1 clove garlic, minced, optional

8 bunches spinach washed and dried

4 cups Veggie Stock, *pages 96 or 97*

1 teaspoon salt

1 teaspoon tarragon

½ teaspoon thyme

½ teaspoon fresh grated nutmeg

1 pint plain yogurt or sour cream

> Heat the ghee in a large pot. Add mustard and cumin seeds and stir until they begin to pop. Add the carrots, celery, onion, garlic and stir. Sauté until translucent.
>
> Add spinach and sauté five minutes. Slowly add 2 or 3 cups stock. Combine well.
>
> Using an immersion blender or food processor, process until smooth. Add more stock to make desired consistency.
>
> Add herbs. Salt to taste.
>
> Serve with dollops of yogurt or sour cream (thin the yogurt or sour cream with water or milk of it is heavier than your soup) and a sprinkling of nutmeg.

Miso Breakfast

Serves 6–8

12-ounce block of firm tofu

8 cups *dashi** or Veggie Stock, *see page 96*

6 tablespoons dark or red miso

2 tablespoons light or white miso

4 scallions, thinly sliced

5 mushrooms, thinly sliced

Lay tofu on a plate between sheets of paper towel. Set a second plate on top and weight with a can or a brick. Leave for 20 minutes to remove liquid from tofu. Cut the tofu into ¼ to ½-inch cubes.

Heat the dashi or veggie stock in a 4-quart saucepan over medium-high heat. When hot, ladle 1 cup into a small bowl. Add the miso, and whisk until smooth.

Bring the remaining dashi or veggie stock to a simmer. Add the miso mixture and whisk to combine. Return to simmer, do not boil. Add the tofu, scallions and mushrooms, and cook for another minute or until heated through.

Remove from the heat, ladle into soup bowls and serve immediately.

*Dashi is Japanese stock, made from kombu (dried kelp), katsuo-bushi (dried bonito flakes), niboshi (dried small sardines), hoshi-shiitake (dried shiitake mushrooms), etc. Kombu dashi and dried shiitake mushroom dashi are known as good vegetarian stocks.

Japanese dashi is best used on the day it's made. Keeps several days if necessary.

Instant dashi powder is also available at stores. It's quick to use dashi powder to make dashi stock. Usually, about 1 teaspoon of dashi powder is used for 2½ cup to 3 cups of water.

Carrot Ginger Bisque

Serves 6–8

8 medium carrots, cut in pieces

1 teaspoon brown mustard seeds

1 teaspoon cumin seeds

3 tablespoons ghee

3 stalks celery, chopped

1 yellow onion, chopped

1 clove garlic, minced

2 inch piece ginger root, peeled and minced or crushed

1 tablespoon Thai-style chili paste

½ teaspoon turmeric

1 teaspoon cinnamon

½ teaspoon cloves

1 teaspoon kosher salt

4–5 cups Veggie Stock, *pages 96 or 97*

1 cup coconut milk

1 pint plain yogurt

Place carrots on a sheet pan lined with parchment. Bake at 350° for about 40 minutes, until cooked through and soft. Set aside.

Add mustard and cumin seeds to soup pot and stir until they begin to pop. Add the ghee. Add carrots, celery, onion, garlic, ginger root, chili paste, cinnamon and cloves and stir.

Add 2 or 3 cups stock. Simmer about 40 minutes. Using an immsersion blender or food processor, blend until smooth. Add more stock to make desired consistency. Add coconut milk to taste. Salt to taste. Serve with dollops of yogurt (thin the yogurt with water or milk of it is heavier than your soup).

Acorn Squash Bisque

Serves 4–6

6 medium acorn squash, cut in half or quarters

3 tablespoons ghee

1 teaspoon brown mustard seeds

1 teaspoon cumin seeds

3 carrots, chopped

3 stalks celery, chopped

1 yellow onion, chopped

1 clove garlic, minced

2 inch piece ginger root, peeled and minced or crushed

1 tablespoon Thai-style chili paste

1 teaspoon cinnamon, ½ teaspoon cloves, 1 teaspoon kosher salt

4–5 cups Veggie Stock, *pages 96 or 97*

1 cup coconut milk

1 pint plain yogurt

Place acorn squash on a sheet pan lined with parchment. Bake at 350° for about 40 minutes, until cooked through and soft. Set aside. When cooled, remove seeds and discard, scoop out pulp and place in a bowl.

Add mustard and cumin seeds to soup pot and dry fry until they begin to pop. Add the ghee. Add carrots, celery, onion, garlic, ginger root, chili paste, cinnamon and cloves and stir. Add the squash pulp and blend well. Add 2 or 3 cups stock. Simmer about 40 minutes.

Using an immersion blender or food processor, blend until smooth. Add more stock to make desired consistency. Add coconut milk to taste. Salt to taste. Heat through.

Serve with dollops of yogurt (thin the yogurt with water or milk of it is heavier than your soup).

Beef and Bacon Stocks and Soups

I don't cook with a lot of beef or pork,

but their are certain things...

Beef Stock

Makes about ½ gallon

4 pounds meaty beef soup bones (beef shanks or short ribs)

3 medium carrots, cut into chunks

3 celery ribs, cut into chunks

2 medium onions, quartered

3 bay leaves

3 garlic cloves

8 to 10 whole peppercorns

3 to 4 sprigs fresh parsley

1 teaspoon dried thyme

1 teaspoon dried marjoram

1 teaspoon dried oregano

8–10 cups water

Plce bones and vegetables in a soup pot. Add warm water to roasting pan; stir to loosen browned bits. Transfer pan juices to Dutch oven. Add seasonings and enough cold water just to cover. Slowly bring to a boil, about 30 minutes.

Reduce heat; simmer, uncovered, 4–5 hours, skimming foam. If necessary, add water during first 2 hours to keep ingredients covered.

Remove beef bones; cool. If desired, remove meat and discard bones; save meat for another use. Strain broth through a cheesecloth-lined colander, discarding vegetables and seasonings. If using immediately, skim fat. Or refrigerate 8 hours or overnight; remove fat from surface.

Broth can be covered and refrigerated up to 3 days or frozen 4–6 months.

Dark Beef Stock

Makes about one gallon

2 pounds beef bones

2 carrots, cut in large chunks

3 celery stalks, cut in large chunks

2 large white onions, quartered

1 head of garlic, halved

1 each rutabaga, parsnip, turnip, halved

2 bay leaves

1 teaspoon salt

4 quarts water

Cover two baking trays with parchment. Place bones on one, the vegetables on the other. Coat with olive oil, salt and herbs. Roast in 350* oven for about an hour.

Remove from oven and Cool to a handling point. Place roasted bones and vegetables in a large stockpot over medium heat. Add about 4 quarts water.

Toss in the bay leaves and salt and allow it to slowly come to a simmer. Lower the heat to medium-low and gently simmer for 3 hours, partially covered.

Be careful not to boil the stock. This causes the protein bits to separate and cloud an otherwise beautiful stock.

Remove from heat and cool slightly before the next step.

Carefully strain the stock through a fine sieve into another pot to remove the solids. Use the stock immediately or to store it. Cover and refrigerate for up to one week or freeze.

Texas Chili Con Carne

Serves 8–10

3 whole sweet fresh or dried New Mexico chilies stems and seeds removed

2 small hot dried chilies like Arbol, stems and seeds removed

3 whole rich fruity dried Ancho or Mulatto chilies, stems and seeds removed

2 whole Chipotle chilies canned in adobo sauce, plus 2 tablespoons sauce, stems and seeds removed

2 quarts Chicken Stock, *pages 49–52*

4 pounds beef chuck, trimmed and cut into thick steaks

Kosher salt and freshly ground black pepper

2 tablespoons vegetable oil

1 large onion, finely diced

4 medium cloves garlic, grated

½ teaspoon powdered cinnamon

1 tablespoon ground cumin

¼ teaspoon ground allspice

2 teaspoons dried oregano

2 tablespoons Asian fish sauce

2 to 3 tablespoons cornmeal masa

2 tablespoons apple cider vinegar

Hot sauce, to taste

Cilantro, chopped onions, scallions, grated cheese, avocado, and warm tortillas for serving as desired

Add dried chiles to large heavy-bottomed Dutch oven or stock pot and cook over medium-high heat, stirring frequently, until slightly darkened with intense, roasted aroma, 2 to 5 minutes. Before they start to smoke, remove chiles to small bowl and set aside.

Transfer chilies and about 1 cup of the chicken stock to food processor and blend (make sure to hold the lid down with a clean kitchen towel or a pot holder to prevent leaking). Blend until smooth, about 1 minute.

Season steaks with salt and pepper. Heat oil in the stock pot to smoke point.

Add half of the beef chuck in a single layer and cook without moving (really, don't, resist the impulse) until browned well, about 6 minutes.

Flip steaks and brown, 3 to 4 more minutes. Transfer steaks to cutting board.

When cool enough to handle, cut seared steaks and raw steaks into approximately 2-inch chunks.

Return pot to heat. Add onions and cook, stirring frequently until translucent and softened, about 2 minutes. Add garlic, cinnamon, cumin, allspice, and oregano, and cook, stirring constantly until fragrant, about 1 minute.

Add all meat back to pan along with chili purée and remaining chicken broth. Stir to combine.

Bring to a boil over high heat, reduce to a simmer, cover, leaving lid ajar and cook, stirring occasionally until meat is completely tender, 2½ to 3 hours. Alternatively, cook in a Dutch oven at 250°F with the lid slightly ajar.

Stir in fish sauce, cornmeal masa, and vinegar.

Add hot sauce to taste. Season to taste with salt.

For best results, cool and store in the refrigerator at least overnight and up to five days. Reheat to serve.

Serve with cilantro, chopped onions, scallions, grated cheese, avocado, and warm tortillas and, traditionally, pinto beans.

French Onion

Much of the success of this soup depends on the stock, and stocks vary tremendously in taste. Depending on your stock, you may need to bump up the flavor with some beef bouillon.

Serves 6–8

6 large red or yellow onions (about 3 pounds), peeled & thinly sliced, about 10 cups

4 tablespoons olive oil

2 tablespoons butter

1 teaspoon sugar

Salt

2 cloves garlic, minced

8 cups Beef stock, Chicken stock, or a combination, *pages 121 or 49–52* (traditionally the soup is made with Beef Stock)

½ cup dry vermouth or dry white wine

2 bay leaves

1 tablespoons (loose) fresh thyme (can also use a few sprigs of fresh thyme) OR ½ teaspoon dried thyme (more to taste)

½ teaspoon freshly ground black pepper

2 tablespoons brandy (optional)

8 slices French bread or baguette cut 1-inch thick

1½ cups grated Swiss Gruyere and a sprinkling of Parmesan

Melt the olive oil and butter in a large pot over medium heat. Add the onions, garlic, bay leaves, thyme and salt and pepper and cook until the onions are very soft and caramelized, about 25 minutes.

Add the wine, bring to a boil, reduce the heat and simmer until the wine has evaporated and the onions are dry, about 5 minutes. Discard the bay leaves and thyme sprigs. Dust the onions with the flour and give them a stir.

Turn the heat down to medium low so the flour doesn't burn, and cook for 10 minutes to cook out the raw flour taste.

Now add the beef broth, bring the soup back to a simmer, and cook for 10 minutes. Season to taste with salt and pepper.

When you're ready to eat, preheat the broiler. Arrange the baguette slices on a baking sheet in a single layer. Sprinkle the slices with the Gruyere and broil until bubbly and golden brown, 3 to 5 minutes.

Ladle the soup in bowls and float several of the Gruyere croutons on top.

Alternative method: Ladle the soup into bowls, top each with 2 slices of bread and top with cheese. Put the bowls into the oven to toast the bread and melt the cheese.

White Bean with Bacon

Serves 4–6

1 pound Great Northern or any white beans

1 pound thick-cut bacon, chopped

1 whole onion, diced

2 whole large carrots, peeled and diced

2 stalks celery, diced

salt and pepper, to taste

4 cloves garlic, minced

2 tablespoons tomato paste

2 whole bay leaves

Minced parsley, to taste

3 whole Roma tomatoes, chopped (optional)

4 cups Dark Chicken Stock, *see page 50*

Pick through the beans and give them a rinse. Put them in a pot and cover with water or extra stock by two inches. Bring to a simmer. Cook 2–3 hours until fairly soft—they will cook an additional half hour in the soup.

Fry the chopped bacon in a soup pot untl crispy and add the onions, carrots, and celery. Season with salt and pepper and cook 3 to 4 minutes. Add the garlic and tomato paste and cook another minute or two. Drain the beans and add to soup pot with three or four cups stock. Add the bay leaf and give it a good stir. Simmer about half an hour or until the beans are thoroughly softened. Add a cup of broth if the liquid level gets too low.

Serve with some reserved chopped bacon, parsley and tomatoes.

Chickpea Stew

Serves 10–12

1 cup dried chickpeas, soaked overnight

2 pounds pork sausages, cooked and cut in pieces

10 cups Beef Stock, *page 121*

2 medium potatoes, peeled and cubed

2 medium bay leaves

1 onion, chopped

3 cloves garlic, chopped

⅓ cup olive oil

1 Butternut squash, peeled and cubed

1 cup green beans

1 bunch Swiss chard, chopped

½ cup bread crumbs

1 ounce almonds

¼ teaspoon saffron

salt and pepper to taste

1 tablespoon red wine vinegar

Place soaked beans, sausages and water in pan. Bring to boil and simmer for 1 hour. Add potatoes and bay leaves and cook for another 30 minutes.

Fry onion and garlic in oil until golden.

Add onion mixture and squash to the stew.

Simmer for 15 minutes. Then add remaining vegetables and simmer for another 15 minutes.

Grind almonds and mix with breadcrumbs. Then add to stew along with saffron.

Season with salt and pepper and simmer 5 minutes. Stir in vinegar and serve.

Potato with Chicken and Bacon

Use baby red, Yukon Gold, or Fingerling potatoes—they'll maintain their shape during cooking.

Serves 6–8

4 bacon slices

2 cups thinly sliced leek (from 2 large leeks)

1 cup sliced carrot (from 2 large carrots)

1 cup sliced celery (from 2 large stalks)

4 cups Dark Chicken Stock, *page 50*

¾ teaspoon kosher salt

½ teaspoon freshly ground black pepper

5 thyme sprigs

12 ounces baby potatoes

2 cups cooked chicken (optional)

>Cook bacon in the oven in a large baking sheet on a piece of parchment 25–30 minutes, until crispy. Remove from pan, reserve fat. Set aside.

>In a pot, heat drippings, then add leek, carrot, and celery. Sauté 5 minutes. Add garlic. Sauté another minute or two.

>Stir in 1 cup stock, scraping pan to loosen browned bits. remaining 3 cups stock, salt, pepper and thyme sprigs to slow cooker. Cover and cook 10 minutes.

>Add potatoes; cover and cook on low for 30 minutes or until potatoes are tender. Add cooked chicken.

>Serve with bacon crumbles on top.

Soup in a Jar

I love delivering warm chicken soup

to an ailing friend or neighbor.

But, what if you could send soup across the country?

Around the world?

Layered Patchwork Mix

Serves 8–10

½ cup barley
½ cup dried split peas
½ cup uncooked white rice
½ cup dry lentils

1 tablespoon dried parsley
1 teaspoon granulated garlic
1 teaspoon ground black pepper
1 teaspoon salt
½ teaspoon garlic powder
1 teaspoon Italian seasoning
1 teaspoon dried sage

In a wide mouth pint jar layer the barley, split peas, rice, and lentils.

In a tiny bag combine the parsley, garlic, pepper, salt, garlic powder, Italian seasoning, and sage.

Decorate the jar lid and attach seasoning packet with ribbon to jar. Attach a recipe card with the following:

Instructions:
To make the soup, empty jar contents into a colander and rinse.
Place contents in a large stockpot and cover with 10 cups water.
Stir in 1 chopped medium onion, and the seasoning packet.
Bring to a boil. Lower heat, cover and simmer for 1 hour, stir occasionally.
Check after 30 minutes and add additional water if necessary.

Rice and Lentils in a Jar

Serves 8–10

2 tablespoons chicken bouillon granules

⅓ cup uncooked rice

⅓ cup red lentils

1 tablespoon dried parsley

½ teaspoon ground black pepper

1 teaspoon poultry seasoning

⅓ cup uncooked rice

⅓ cup green lentils

Measure the chicken bouillon granules into a 1 pint jar.

Top with ⅓ cup of rice, red lentils, dried parsley, pepper, poultry seasoning, ⅓ cup of rice and then the green lentils on top.

Seal with a lid and ring. Attach recipe card with the following:

Instructions:

To make the soup, bring 2 teaspoons butter and 8 cups water to a boil in a large pot. Pour in the contents of the jar and add ¼ cup chopped celery and 1 cup cooked chicken.

Simmer until the lentils are tender, about 30 minutes.

Ginna BB Gordon

Garden Vegetable Mix in a Jar

Serves 6–8

¼ cup red kidney beans

¾ cup dehydrated vegetable mix

¼ cup pot barley

¼ cup wild rice

¼ cup vegetable orzo

¼ cup black beans

¼ cup vegetable bouillon

1 tablespoon onion flakes

½ tablespoon parsley flakes

1 tsp thyme

In a pint size jar, layer first five ingredients as listed above.

In a small bowl mix remaining ingredients until well combined.

Place spice mix in a small plastic bag or wrap well in plastic wrap to keep separate. Place spice pack on top of beans.

Seal jar. Decorate, label and include cooking instructions.

Instructions:

To make the soup, remove spice pack.

Pour remaining contents of jar into fine mesh sieve, rinse well.

Place in soup pot. Add spices and 7 cups water, simmer for 10 minutes

Reduce heat. Add 1 cup diced tomatoes.

Cover and simmer for 1–1½ hours. Adjust seasoning and garnish with parsley. Add leftover veggies or meat from your fridge.

Chicken Noodle Mix in a Jar

Serves 6–8

1 cup small pasta

1 cup dehydrated vegetable mix

2½ tablespoon chicken bouillon

½ teaspoon ground black pepper

¼ teaspoon thyme

⅛ teaspoon celery seeds

⅛ teaspoon garlic powder

1 tablespoon onion flakes

½ tablespoon parsley

½ tablespoon chives

⅛ teaspoon hot pepper flakes (optional)

In a pint jar, layer pasta and dehydrated vegetables.

In a small bowl mix remaining ingredients until well combined.

Pour herbs and spices on top of final layer. Seal jar.

Decorate and label. Include cooking instructions.

Instructions:

To make the soup, combine entire contents of jar with 8 cups water in large soup pot. Bring to boil.

Cover, reduce heat and simmer for 20 minutes.

Stir in 3 cups diced, cooked chicken and simmer an additional 5 minutes.

Bean Mix in a Jar

Serves 6–8

¼ cup each red lentils, black eyed peas, black beans, green lentils, red beans, pinto beans, green split peas

1 teaspoon dried basil

1 tablespoon dried parsley

1 tablespoon dried onion flakes

½ teaspoon garlic powder

2 tablespoon beef or vegetable bouillon

1 bay leaf

In a pint jar, layer beans and peas in order listed above.

In a small bowl mix remaining ingredients until well combined.

Place spice mix in a small bag.

Place spice pack on top of beans and peas.

Seal jar, decorate, label and include cooking instructions.

Instructions:

To make the soup, remove spice pack. Empty ingredients of jar into the soup pot. Rinse well and drain.

Add 6 cups water and bring to boil. Remove from heat and let stand for 1 hour. Drain, rinse, drain again.

Add 7 cups water, 1 cup diced tomatoes and the spice mix. Bring to boil.

Reduce heat and simmer for 1 hour. Adjust seasoning to taste, remove bay leaf and garnish with fresh parsley.

Things to go with Soup

Legendary Cream Scones

Makes about a dozen

3 cups organic, unbleached pastry flour

3 teaspoons baking powder

½ teaspoon salt

1 tablespoon baker's superfine sugar

2 sticks unsalted butter, cut in pieces

4 eggs

⅔ cup heavy cream

⅔ cup sour cream

Preheat oven to 350°

Sift dry ingredients. Beat eggs, cream and sour cream together in a separate bowl.

Place dry ingredients and cold butter in food processor and process until mixture looks and feels like coarse meal, less than a minute.

Add egg and cream mixture and flavor*; quickly mix together until dough forms a soft ball.

Scoop out about one cup of dough for each scone onto sheet pan covered with parchment. Sprinkle with sugar (optional).

Bake about 20 minutes, or until golden and cooked through.

*2 tablespoons lemon zest, dried fruit or savory herbs.

Flatbread Crackers

Makes about a dozen

3 cups flour

2 teaspoons baking powder

2 teaspoons salt

1 stick unsalted butter, cut in pieces

1 cup plain yogurt

1 cups sesame seeds, toasted

Glaze:

2 large eggs

2 tablespoons sugar

1 tablespoon Bragg's Liquid Aminos or soy sauce

Preheat oven to 325°

In food processor, mix flour, baking powder and salt. Add butter and grind coarsely. Transfer to a large bowl and add yogurt and one cup of the sesame seeds. Mix to form a dough. Wrap in plastic and chill for 30 minutes.

Stir eggs, sugar and Bragg's together. Set aside. Divide the dough into quarters. Divide each quarter into 12 pieces. Rolling the dough, make 4 inch logs with your hands. Roll out each log with a floured rolling pin into a strip about 12 x 4 inches.

Carefully transfer to a baking sheet covered with parchment. Brush strips with glaze and sprinkle with remaining seeds.

Bake crackers two sheets at a time, rotating upper and lower, 20 minutes max, until glaze is golden and crackers look crisp but not hard.

Transfer to cooling rack while you continue rolling and baking.

Stores for about a week in airtight containers.

Sourdough Crackers

Makes a lot

3 cups white flour

1 teaspoon sea salt

1 ½ cups sourdough starter "discard," fed

1 stick unsalted butter, melted

Olive oil for brushing

Coarse salt (such as kosher or sea salt) for sprinkling on top

Preheat the oven to 300°F. Mix together one cup flour, 1 teaspoon salt and melted butter to make a sort of roux. Add in the starter and more flour to make a smooth (not sticky), cohesive dough. Shape into a small rectangular slab. Dust with flour and cover with parchment and refrigerate for 30 minutes, until the dough is firm. Remove dough from fridge for about ½ an hour before making crackers.

Very lightly flour a piece of parchment, your rolling pin, and the top of the dough. Cut dough into four equal pieces. Keep dusting with flour. Roll each piece on parchment to about 1/16" thick. The dough will have ragged, uneven edges; that's OK. Just try to make it thin. Lightly brush with oil and sprinkle the coarse salt over the top. Cut the dough into even squares; a rolling pizza wheel works well here. Transfer the dough and parchment together onto a baking sheet.

Bake two trays of crackers at a time at 300° for 15 minutes. Reverse the baking sheets: both top to bottom, and front to back; this will help the crackers brown evenly. Bake another 15 minutes or until light golden brown. (While the first two trays are baking, roll out the next two pieces of dough onto parchment.)

When fully browned, remove from the oven, slide crackers and parchment onto cutting board to cool. Place second sets of cracker dough on parchment onto baking sheets and repeat baking. I put the perfect crackers in a ½ gallon jar and leave the ragged edges on the counter. They are usually gone in ten minutes.

Store airtight at room temperature for up to a week; in the freeze for longer storage.

Oatmeal Bread

Makes 2 large or 4 small loaves

Baking spray

2 cups oatmeal, either rolled or steel cut

4 cups boiling water

8 oz. Dark molasses

2 tablespoons melted butter

1 cup dry milk

3 tablespoons yeast

1 teaspoon salt

4 cups wheat flour

4 cups white flour

Place oatmeal in large mixing bowl, pour boiling water over and stir. Let cool for about two hours or overnight. Dissolve yeast in ¼ cup lukewarm water. To oatmeal, add molasses, melted butter, dry milk, dissolved yeast. Mix well. Let stand fifteen minutes. Add salt and begin adding flour, a little at a time, alternating between wheat and white to achieve a soft but firm dough. You may not need all eight cups flour.

Cover bowl and let rise for several hours, until doubled in bulk. Punch down and roll out onto floured board. Knead and shape into loaves.

Place dough into well sprayed baking pans and let rise again, until dough comes over top of pans.

Preheat oven to 350°.

Bake for approximately 40 minutes. When inserted knife or skewer comes out clean, it's done!

(Cracked wheat or left over cooked oatmeal can also be used. If using cooked oatmeal, omit the 4 cups of boiling water.)

French Bread

Makes two baguettes or one large loaf

2 tablespoons active dry yeast

2 tablespoons sugar

4 cups lukewarm water

8 cups sifted white flour

1 teaspoon salt

In a large bowl, dissolve the yeast and sugar in lukewarm water. Let stand for two minutes.

Stir in half the flour and the salt.

Add just enough of the remaining flour to hold the dough together—it will form soft, slightly sticky dough.

Knead in the bowl for about five minutes, adding just enough more flour to assist kneading and not stick to your hands.

Cover and let rise until double, 1–2 hours.

Set near a warm oven or fire to quicken the rising process.

Preheat the oven to 400°.

When the dough has risen, punch it down with your hand and divide into loaves: two medium loaf pans, two baguette pans or one large loaf pan. A clay pan will produce a great crust.

Let rise again for ½ hour to 45 minutes, or until the dough has risen over the top of the pan(s).

Bake for about forty minutes on the middle rack. Place trays of water on the rack below. The loaves will be brown and crusty when they are done. Pierce with skewer for doneness—if they come out clean, that's that!

Cool for one hour before slicing.

Ginna BB Gordon

Dumplings

Makes about one dozen

2 cups flour

1½ teaspoon salt

1 tablespoon baking powder

2 tablespoons vegetable oil

1 cup warm water

2 cups broth

Chopped chives or parsley for garnish if desired

Combine flour, salt and baking powder.

Add oil and water and mix until smooth.

Add a bit more water until dumplings are soft and not at all dry.

Bring broth to a boil and add dumplings by spoonful.

Reduce heat and cook dumplings 4–5 minutes.

(Do in batches if you are using a small pan.)

Serve dumplings in broth or soup garnished with chopped parsley or chives as desired.

Warm Wild Rice Salad

Serves 6–8

3 cups cooked wild and brown rice mix, cooled slightly

2 avocados, cut in bite sized pieces

1 cup fresh fennel bulb, diced

2 tablespoons fennel seeds

1 cup celery, diced

½ cup dried blueberries

¼ cup sunflower seeds

¼ cup raisins

¼ cup chopped fresh dill

¼ cup chopped fresh chives

1 cup fresh or frozen corn, sautéed in ghee and cooled

Salt & pepper to taste

Lemon-lime Dressing

    Combine all ingredients in a bowl and serve at slightly above room temperature.

Lemon-Lime Dressing

1 tablespoon olive oil

Agave or honey to taste

1 tablespoon lemon juice

¼–½ cup lime juice

    Combine all ingredients in a jar and shake well.

Banana Bread
Gluten, Sugar & Dairy Free

Makes one loaf

2¼ cups almond flour

1 teaspoon salt

1 teaspoon baking soda

1 teaspoon baking powder

2 tablespoons stevia

½ cup raisins

2 ripe bananas, mashed

1 tablespoon cinnamon

3 eggs, separated

2 tablespoons ghee

Beat egg whites until stiff. Mix the dry ingredients with the wet ingredients, alternately, then fold in egg whites.

Bake in a sprayed bread pan or muffin tin for 40 minutes or until golden.

Cool before slicing.

Variations:

Sweet Potato Bread

Exchange 2 cups mashed cooked sweet potatoes for the bananas

Carrot Apple Cake

Exchange two cups roasted smashed carrots for the banana
(Roast carrots and apples in melted butter and salt to bring out the sweetness)

Compound Butters

Make Compounds with room temperature butter and a handful of herbs, or add shallots (minced or sautéed), honey, maple syrup, pesto. Compound butters add flavor to meats, soups, breads and biscuits.

Example:

Sun Dried Tomato Butter

1 cup unsalted butter
4 tablespoons chopped fresh parsley
1 teaspoon minced garlic
1 ounce sun-dried tomatoes, chopped
Salt and pepper to taste

In a mixing bowl, cream the butter.
Mix in parsley, garlic, and tomatoes.
Use melon ballers to makes rounds.
Chill for at least 2 hours.

Fruit Soups

Cherry

Serves 4–6

1 pound pitted sour cherries
2 cups water
1 cup red wine
¼ cup sugar
¼ teaspoon orange zest
1 teaspoon cornstarch

Whipping cream

    Cook about ten minutes. Serve hot or cold with whipped cream.

Mixed Fruit

Serves 6–8

½ cantaloupe, seeds removed
1 cup fresh pineapple
1 cup peaches
1 cup Granny Smith apples, peeled and diced
2 cups strawberries
¼ cup sugar
2 tablespoons honey
2 cups water
¼ cup pineapple juice
¼ cup lemon juice
¼ cup orange juice
Sour cream, for garnish
Orange rind, for garnish

Combine the fruit in a soup pot with the sugar and honey.

Add water, pineapple, lemon and orange juice.

Simmer uncovered for 15 minutes or until fruit is soft.

Allow fruit to cool. With an immersion blender, blend until smooth. Chill.

Garnish servings with a dollop of sour cream and orange rind.

Ginna BB Gordon

Mother Sauces

Espagnole

Brown Sauce

Makes about four cups

⅓ cup chopped lean bacon

¼ cup butter

1 small onion, chopped

1 small carrot, diced

1 shallot, sliced

½ cup flour

2½ cups Dark Chicken Stock, *page 50*

1 cup chopped mushrooms

1 teaspoon tomato paste

1 teaspoon sherry

Bouquet Garni

salt and pepper

Sauté bacon in butter. Add vegetables and sauce for 5 minutes.

Stir in flour. Let the flour brown, cooking slowly for about 30 minutes. Stir occasionally. Don't let it scorch.

Stir in stock and mushrooms and Garni. Simmer 30 minutes.

Add tomato paste and sherry. Simmer 15 minutes.

Strain the sauce.

Good for freezing.

Béchamel

White sauce with veggies

Makes about three cups

2½ cups milk
1 onion, peeled
6 cloves
pinch of mace
5 peppercorns
1 small carrot
1 bay leaf
1 parsley sprig
3 tablespoons butter
⅓ cup flour
salt and pepper

Press the cloves into the onion and place in a saucepan.

Add the milk, mace, carrot, bay leaf and parsley to simmer for 15 minutes.

Let stand for 15 minutes off the heat and then strain.

Melt the butter in a saucepan and stir in the flour. Cook, stirring, one minute.

Remove pan from heat and begin adding warm milk while constantly stirring.

When all milk is added, beat well for a smooth sauce.

Use the warm milk without additions for a plain white sauce.

Velouté

Makes about three cups

2 tablespoons butter
¼ cup flour
2½ cups Veggie Stock, *see page 96*
mushrooms or trimmings
parsley
½ tablespoons cream
salt and pepper

Melt the butter, add the flour, cook, the roux while stirring for 2 minutes.

Slowly add stock and bring to a boil.

Add mushrooms and some parsley sprigs.

Reduce by half by simmering for about one hour.

Strain and return to saucepan.

Stir in cream.

Season to taste.

Tomato

Makes about two cups

1 onion, chopped
½ cup chopped bacon
1 carrot, diced
2 tablespoons olive oil
3 tablespoons flour
1½ pounds fresh tomatoes
1 cup Veggie or Chicken Stock, *see pages 96 or 50*
bay leaf
parsley
basil
salt and pepper

Place bacon, onion and carrot into a saucepan and cook for five minutes.

While stirring, add the flour.

Add remaining ingredients, bring to a simmer and cook for one hour.

Cool and strain.

Good for freezing.

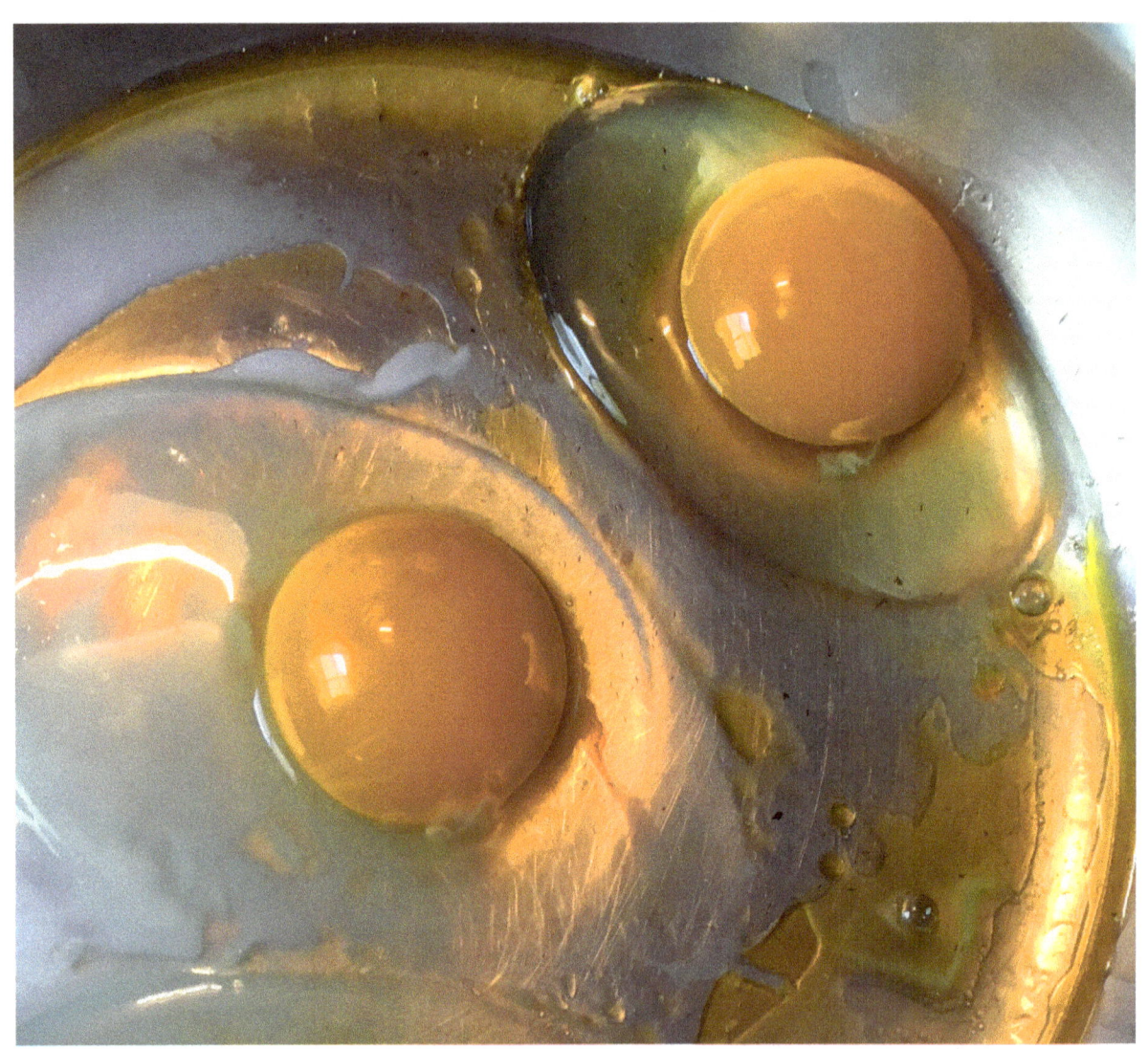

Emulsions

Basic Mayonnaise

Makes 1½ cups

1¼ cups light olive oil
1 large egg
½ teaspoon mustard powder or Dijon Mustard
½ teaspoon salt
Juice of ½ lemon

> Always begin with room temperature ingredients.
>
> Place ¼ cup of the olive oil, the egg, mustard, and salt in a blender, food processor, or mixing bowl.
>
> Mix thoroughly.
>
> While the food processor or blender is running (or while mixing in a bowl with an immersion blender), slowly drizzle in the remaining 1 cup olive oil.
>
> After you've added all the oil and the mixture has emulsified, add the lemon juice, blending on low or stirring to incorporate.

Hollandaise

Makes about one cup

4 egg yolks
1 tablespoon freshly squeezed lemon juice
1 stick unsalted butter, melted
Pinch cayenne
Pinch salt

Vigorously whisk the egg yolks and lemon juice together in a stainless steel bowl and until the mixture is thickened and doubled in volume.

Place the bowl over a saucepan (or use a double boiler) of simmering water, with the water not touching the bottom of the bowl.

Keep whisking.

Don't let the eggs get too hot or they will scramble.

Slowly drizzle in the melted butter and whisk until thickened and doubled in volume.

Remove from heat, whisk in cayenne and salt.

Cover and place in a warm spot until ready to use.

Misc

Tomatillo Sauce

Makes about two cups

3 tablespoons olive oil

1 teaspoon cumin, seeds or ground

1 small onion, chopped

1 pound tomatillos, de-papered and cut in half

2 cloves garlic, smashed

2 or more tablespoons brown sugar, depending on the sweetness of the tomatillos

    Heat olive oil in a medium soup pot or sauce pan. Sauté onion for five minutes. Add garlic and sauté another five minutes.

    Add tomatillos and cook until very tender, about 40 minutes.

    Add brown sugar and cook another ten minutes. Blend with immersion blender, or cool and blend in food processor.

That's it, baby.

Enchilada Sauce

Makes 12 cups

8 dried Ancho chilies

2 gallons boiling water or

2 cups roasted fresh red Ancho/Poblano chilies

⅓ cup vegetable oil

4 cups each, chopped:

carrots, onions, celery

About 1½ gallons Veggie or Dark Chicken Stock, *see pages 96 or 50*

½ to 1 cup cornmeal

1–2 teaspoons ground cumin

salt and pepper to taste

    Place dried chilies in boiling water and turn off the heat.

    Soak about three hours or overnight.

    Drain, cool, stem and seed the chilies. Leave the skins on.

    Or, proceed with roasted chilies by seeding.

    In a large stock-pot sauté vegetables in hot oil until soft.

    Add chilies and stock. Simmer 20 minutes.

    Blend well.

    Thicken with cornmeal. Season with cumin, salt and pepper.

    This makes a lot. Can be frozen.

"Curry" Sauce

For an explanation of the word curry, *see page 16.*

Serves 4–6

GB's Dry Curry Blend

2 tablespoons coriander seeds

1 tablespoon cumin seeds

2 teaspoons black or yellow mustard seeds

1 teaspoon black peppercorns

½ teaspoon whole cloves

12 to 15 dried red cayenne chiles (like chiles de arbol), stems discarded

1 teaspoon ground turmeric

Sauce

2 tablespoons vegetable oil

1 small onion, coarsely chopped

4 medium-size cloves garlic, coarsely chopped

4 pieces fresh ginger, coarsely chopped

(each about the size and thickness of a 25-cent coin; no need to peel the skin),

2 teaspoons GB's Blend (above)

½ cup diced tomatoes with their juices

½ cup half-and-half

1½ pounds skinless, boneless chicken breasts, cut into 2-inch cubes

1 teaspoon coarse kosher or sea salt

2 tablespoons finely chopped fresh cilantro leaves and tender stems

Spice Blend

Place the coriander, cumin, mustard seeds, peppercorns, cloves, and chiles in a spice grinder (you can also use a coffee grinder) and grind them to the consistency of finely ground black pepper. Stir in the turmeric, which will yellow the spice blend with its characteristic sunny bright disposition. Store the spice blend in a tightly sealed container, away from excess light, heat, and humidity, for up to 3 months.

Sauce

Heat the oil in a large skillet over medium-high heat. Add the onion, garlic, and ginger and fry until the onion edges are light brown, 4 to 5 minutes.

Sprinkle the spice blend into the skillet and stir. Let the spices roast in the onion medley about 10 seconds. Pour in the tomatoes and stir. Lower the heat and simmer the sauce uncovered, stirring occasionally, until the tomato pieces soften and moisture evaporates, 5 to 7 minutes.

Pour the half-and-half into the skillet and scrape the bottom to release bits of onion, garlic and ginger, deglazing the skillet and releasing flavors back into the sauce. Purée the curry until it is smooth.

Return the sauce to the skillet and stir in the chicken and salt. Simmer the curry, covered, over medium-low heat, stirring occasionally, until the chicken is cooked through, 12 to 15 minutes.

Sprinkle the cilantro on top of the chicken curry and serve.

Red Lentil Dahl

Serves 6-8

1 cup dried red lentils
Pinch of salt

2 tablespoons ghee
1 tablespoons mustard seeds
1 teaspoon cumin seeds
1 teaspoon ground coriander
1 teaspoon turmeric
1 one inch piece fresh ginger root, grated
1 cup diced carrots
2 stalks celery, diced
2 leeks, washed and chopped and washed again and drained
1 cup currants or raisins, chopped, optional
2-3 cups Veggie Stock, *page 96*

1 cup fresh chopped cilantro
Yogurt

> Add mustard and cumin seeds to the soup pot. Dry fry one minute to release flavor. Add the ghee, coriander and turmeric and stir.
>
> Add carrots, celery, leeks and raisins and stir. Sauté until translucent.
>
> Slowly add 2 or 3 cups stock. Blend well.
>
> Add red lentils and simmer until just cooked through, about 40 minutes. Add more stock to make desired consistency.
>
> Salt to taste. Serve with dollops of yogurt (thin the yogurt with water or milk of it is heavier than your soup).
>
> Serve with seedy rice and chutney or salsa.

Ginna BB Gordon

Afterword & Acknowledgements

A good collaboration makes my heart go pitter pat. Unlike art by committee (which spells d.i.s.a.s.t.e.r.), an art collaboration brings more to the table than the sum of the parts of the collaborators. Each contribution is filled with combined creative juices and enthusiasms, a cosmic fertilizer. The project sprouts wings, like cotyledon leaves, the first to emerge on a seedling.

One day in the spring of 2019, in the front row of one of David's *Historic Jacksonville* concerts, I spoke to our friend, Gates, about *The Soup Kit*. I described my desire to find a variety of decorative papers, bowls and spoons for photos. She said, as we settled down and David tuned his guitar for the first song, "I think you should pay me a visit on the hill." What a find! All decorative papers, Bakelite spoons and ceramic bowls are from the Gates McKibbin private collection.

Gates also deserves a thank you for being a stellar first reader of all my endeavors with the written word. Her eyes see more clearly than do mine, all starry as they are.

Most herbs and flowers in *The Soup Kit* grew in my plot of dirt, but Chef Dana Mitchell of Ashland, Oregon, provided an abundance of photo-worthy garden growth, including onion, chive and garlic flowers, marigolds and zinneas.

Melissa Lofton came to visit one day and, by the end of the next day, had painted a brand new tropical island for our kitchen, which has become the colorful backdrop for all culinary creations. I look at those beautiful leaves and bugs and butterflies and thank her every day.

My mother, Virginia, provided so much talent and discovery in the culinary and art realms, it is hard to succinctly say thank you to her in print. From the crib, I smelled cinnamon and cardamom, incense in the temple of sustenance. Her breads sustained us all right, and other aromas wafted through the Big House at Bonnebrook Farm: burbling stock, sweet peaches in syrup, cherry pie, soup.

As Your Garden Grows, a little farm in Medford, Oregon, operated by two young women, Aisha and Kelsey, provided the carrots for the knife cuts as well as the eclectic collection of fresh eggs for the Mise en Place photo. Those carrots looked good, and tasted divine later in **Carrot Ginger Soup**.

The most poignant acknowledgement goes to the late Lee Gardner, dear friend and maker of exotic hardwood cutting boards. When Lee died in 2018, his wife, Jacki, presented me with one of his few remaining boards, which became an important part of *The Soup Kit* photo shoots.

And, always, David, my main man, my squeeze, my soup taster and companion, deserves the standing ovation. Yes, he reaps the rewards of all my culinary activity, but he also washes sink loads of dishes and puts up with myriad messes throughout any given day. And sings to me while I make dinner. And is my personal typographer and fellow book designer. He rocks. Or maybe I should say, he spoons.

Make soup. Make it yourself. Learn how to make crackers and bread and culinary spice mixtures so you can fill your home with savory incense and your tummies with wholesome goodness. I thank you, too, for reading *The Soup Kit* and making it a part of your kitchen.

~ Ginna BB Gordon

About Ginna

Ginna BB Gordon has owned businesses (Ginna's Café, The Book Studio, and Ginna & Co.) and managed kitchens and cafés in other folks' businesses (Rainbow Ranch, Calistoga, CA; Chopra Center for Well Being, La Jolla, CA; the Thunderbird Bookshop & Café and the Cornucopia Café & Market, both in Carmel, CA).

She has also managed large-scale special events for non-profits (Carmel Music Society; Carmel Bach Festival; American Tall Ship Institute) and for many private clients (including Steven Seagal at his home in Southern California, where Tibetan monks roamed the halls and created fire pujas in the backyard while Ginna prepped dinner for six, or eight or 20, depending upon the star's whim).

Throughout her busy 30-year career in the food and event business, Ginna has entertained herself and friends with art and garden parties, ceramic workshops, gifts from the garden and kitchen and herbal products for the body and table. Ginna is a dedicated Maker, DIY Artist and Upcycler.

Ginna has (so far) authored four books about cooking: *A Simple Celebration – the Nutritional Program for the Chopra Center for Well Being* (Random House/Harmony Books 1997); *Bonnebrook* and *The Gingerbread Farm*, glimpses of the many teachers and styles of cooking Ginna experienced on her journey as a retreat cook and café chef; and *First You Grow the Pumpkin*, which shares favorite tricks for growing, preserving and creating in the kitchen. *The Soup Kit* continues this "how to" series.

Ginna studied Ayurveda and the Ayurvedic cooking style with Drs. Deepak Chopra, David Simon and Shamali Joshi.

Her studies in the arts included UCLA Interior Design, the Guild of the Books Arts Carmel, Monterey Peninsula College and privately with myriad artists in and around California, including Alison Stillwell Cameron (Chinese calligraphy), Tulku Jamyang Rinpoche (Tibetan thangka painting) and Louisa Jenkins (collage).

Currently, Ginna and her husband, singer, lecturer and author David Gordon (www.spiritsound.com), are partners in Lucky Valley Press, offering editing, design and prepress services to independent authors. (www.luckyvalleypress.com)

When Ginna is not cooking, writing (sometime, ask her about her novel series), or digging in the dirt, she builds tiny shrines, upcycles paraphernalia otherwise on the way to the "heave-ho heap," knits afghans and enjoys myriad other homey tasks and studio arts. (blog.ginna.com).

Measurements & Conversions

Measurement Abbreviations

tsp = teaspoon	c = cup	sm = small
Tbsp = tablespoon	pt = pint	lg = large
fl = fluid	qt = quart	ml = milliliter
oz = ounce	gal = gallon	g = gram
pkg = package	lb = pound	kg = kilogram

Pinches to Spoons

1 pinch = 0.5 gram = less than ⅛ teaspoon

1 dash = 1.18 grams = 3 drops = .003 teaspoon water

1 milliliter (ml) = 1 cubic centimeter (cc)

1 teaspoon = 4.73 grams = ⅙ ounce of water

1 tablespoon = 14.18 grams = 3 teaspoons water

4 tablespoons = 56.70 grams = ¼ cup water

16 tablespoons = 226.80 gram = 1 cup water

Gallons to Liters

1 gal = 4 qt = 8 pts = 16 cups = 128 fl oz = 3.79 L

½ gal = 2 qt = 4 pts = 8 cups = 64 fl oz = 1.89 L

¼ gal = 1 qt = 2 pts = 4 cups = 32 fl oz = 0.95 L

½ qt = 1 pt = 2 cups = 16 fl oz = 0.47 L

¼ qt = pt = 1 cup = 8 fl oz = 0.24 L

Fluid Ounces to Liters

1 fl oz = 29.63 ml

1 cup = 237.00 ml

1 pint = 474.00 ml

1 quart = 0.95 liter

1 gallon = 3.79 liters

Milliliters to Gallons

1 ml = 0.04 fl oz

50 ml = 1.70 fl oz

500 ml = 2.13 cups

1 liter = 1.06 quarts

10 liters = 2.64 gallons

°F–°C Conversions

-10°F = -20°C	-18°C = 0°F
0°F = -18°C	0°C = 32°F
32°F = 0°C	5°C = 41°F
68°F = 20°C	10°C = 50°F
90°F = 32°C	20°C = 68°F
212°F = 100°C	30°C = 86°F
300°F = 149°C	50°C = 122°F
350°F = 177°C	60°C = 140°F
400°F = 204°C	100°C = 212°F
450°F = 232°C	150°C = 302°F
500°F = 260°C	200°C = 482°F

Grams to Pounds

1 gram = 0.04 ounces

1 kilogram = 2.2 pounds

5 kilograms = 11.01 pounds

20 kilograms = 44.03 pounds

1 metric ton = 1.10 tons

Ounces to Kilograms

1 ounce = 28.35 grams

16 ounces = 1 pound = 453.60 grams

5 pounds = 2.27 kilograms

25 pounds = 11.34 kilograms

1 ton = 0.91 metric tons

Cups to Spoons

1 tablespoon (Tbsp) = 3 teaspoons (tsp)
1/16 cup (c) = 1 Tbsp
1/8 cup = 2 Tbsp
1/6 cup = 2 Tbsp + 2 tsp
1/4 cup = 4 Tbsp
1/3 cup = 5 Tbsp + 1 tsp
3/8 cup = 6 Tbsp
1/2 cup = 8 Tbsp
2/3 cup = 10 Tbsp + 2 tsp
3/4 cup = 12 Tbsp
1 cup = 16 Tbsp
1 cup = 48 Tbsp

Cups to Gallons

1 cup = 8 fluid ounces (fl oz)
2 cups = 1 pint (pt)
2 pints = 1 quart (qt) = 32 fl oz
4 cups = 1 quart
8 cups = 64 fl oz
1 gallon (gal) = 4 quarts = 128 fl oz

Inches to Kilometers

1 inch (in or ") = 2.54 centimeters
4 inches = 10.16 cm
1 foot = 0.30 meter
5 feet = 1.52 meters
10 feet = 3.05 meters
1 yard = 0.91 meters
1 mile = 1.6 km
50 miles = 80.47 km

Centimeters to Miles

1 cm = 0.39 inches
2.54 cm = 1 inch
5 cm = 1.97 inches
1 meter = 3.28 feet = 1.09 yards
15 meters = 49.21 feet
1 km = 0.62 mile
1500 meters = 4921.25 feet
50 km = 31.07 mi

Dish Measurements

9x13 inch baking dish = 22x33 cm baking dish

8x8 inch baking dish = 20x20 cm baking dish

9x5 inch loaf pan = 23x12 cm loaf pan = 8 cups = 2 liters

10 inch tart or cake pan = 25 cm tart or cake pan

9 inch cake pan = 22 cm cake pan

Bar Drink Measurements

1 dash = 6 drops

3 teaspoons = 1 ounce

1 pony = 1 ounce

1 jigger = 1 ounce

1 large jigger = 2 ounces

1 std. whiskey glass = 2 ounces

1 pint = 16 fluid ounces

1 fifth = 25.6 fluid ounces

1 quart = 32 fluid ounces

Notes

www.ingramcontent.com/pod-product-compliance
Lightning Source LLC
Chambersburg PA
CBHW061753290426
44108CB00029B/2980